Playing with

STENCILS

Playing with STENCILS

Exploring Repetition, Pattern, and Personal Designs

Quarry Books
100 Cummings Center, Suite 406L
Beverly, MA 01915

quarrybooks.com • craftside.typepad.com

© 2013 by Quarry Books
Text © 2013 Amy Rice
Photography © 2013 Amy Rice

First published in the United States of America in 2013 by
Quarry Books, a member of
Quayside Publishing Group
100 Cummings Center
Suite 406-L
Beverly, Massachusetts 01915-6101
Telephone: (978) 282-9590
Fax: (978) 283-2742
www.quarrybooks.com
Visit www.Craftside.Typepad.com for a behind-the-scenes
peek at our crafty world!

10 9 8 7 6 5 4 3 2 1

ISBN: 978-1-59253-829-4

Digital edition published in 2013
eISBN: 978-1-61058-774-7

Library of Congress Cataloging-in-Publication Data

Rice, Amy.
  Playing with stencils : exploring repetition, pattern, and personal designs /
Amy Rice.
      pages cm – (Playing)
    ISBN 978-1-59253-829-4 (pbk.)
    I. Title.
  TT270.R49 2013
  745.7'3–dc23

                        2012037756

Design: Studioink - www.studioink.co.uk
Cover Images: Amy Rice
Templates: Amy Rice

Printed in China

Contents

Introduction

A stencil is simply a template used to repeat the same drawing, pattern, or shape over and over. Stenciling is one of the oldest art techniques known to man. Prehistoric peoples used their own hands as stencils in cave paintings. There is evidence of stencils being used in ancient Egypt and China. In the Renaissance, stencils were used to reproduce playing cards as well as the very first flocked wallpaper. In colonial America, the high prices of fancy European household goods inspired American crafters to develop a stencil form and style still recognizable today.

By the 1800s, manufacturers of household goods were using stencils in mass-produced items. This continued until the early 1900s when silk screening replaced stenciling in most commercial applications.

The Art Deco era of the 1930s and '40s witnessed a resurgence of stencil use and design, but as other print methods were developed and advanced, stenciling fell out of favor. The 1970s craft movement brought stencils back to the forefront for use in interior design and in arts and crafts.

Although there are examples of stencils being used in graffiti art as early as the late 1960s, the early 1980s was when the movement really began to pick up momentum. Today, there is a worldwide subculture of graffiti stencil artists that has inspired books, magazine articles, and films. Some of these artists exhibit in well-respected galleries and museums. Regardless of one's opinion on the validity of street art, it is undeniable that the street art stencil movement has raised the bar significantly for stencil design. What was considered a complicated cut or design ten years ago is now simple and common.

The current DIY craft movement is just another force moving the ancient art and craft technique of stenciling to new levels. Consumer interest has led to new tools and techniques that make stenciling easier than it ever was. This new technology, coupled with literally thousands of years and dozens of cultural traditions of stencil designs to be inspired by, make it a fantastic time to cut a stencil.

01.

Designing, Enlarging, Transferring, Cutting, and Burning

Designing a Stencil

This book includes fourteen stencil template designs (page 126) to use on your own projects. I've included directions for how to enlarge your stencils (if needed), as well as how to cut a design into a stencil that can be used again and again. Using the stencil templates included in the book first will help you better understand what does and does not work in a stencil design when you are turning your own art or design into a custom stencil.

○ Shape stencil

○ Line stencil

Designing a stencil is rewarding and can be either simple or challenging. There are two basic stencil designs that will be covered in this book—shape stencils and line drawing stencils—but I will also touch on two variations of these, including reverse stencils and repeating pattern stencils.

A stencil works by letting the art medium (various forms of paint and pigment) through only certain parts of the stencil to create the desired design. A shape stencil is a silhouette, a simple and easily recognizable form. This is the easiest type of stencil to design and when properly used can have dynamic results in spite of its simplicity.

A line drawing stencil is a bit more complicated, but once the basics are understood, any drawing or image can be turned into a stencil. Think about the letter "O" as a simple line drawing. If you were to cut around the outside of the circle that comprises an "O," what would be left would be a circle or round hole, not an "O." To make an "O," bridges must be used. A stenciled "O" is generally two half "O"s. The small spaces between the two half "O"s are called bridges.

○ Sometimes the shape stencil and the line stencil can
be used together, as shown here.
○ Line and shape stencil together

○ Start with a simple line drawing.

○ Next, use correction fluid to make periodic "bridges".

○ If you can make a continuous line to every section of your drawing, it will work as a stencil.

○ Studying a deck of stencil letters readily available at most hardware stores is a good way to understand how bridges are used in stencils.

PRACTICE

Take a plain white piece of paper and with a black pen make a simple line drawing (A). When that is complete, use white correction fluid to make bridges periodically throughout your drawing (B). Next, take a pencil and without ever lifting the pencil off the page and without ever crossing a black line, make a pencil path to every section of the drawing (C). If that is not possible, it will not work as a stencil and more bridges will need to be added until the pencil task is doable for the stencil to work.

VARIATIONS ON LINE AND SHAPE STENCILS

There are two common variations on the line and shape stencils that can be used to produce beautiful designs. A reverse stencil is just what it sounds like: instead of applying paint on the inside of a cutout design, you apply the paint or pigment on the outside of a solid design. Here's a simple example: prehistoric peoples applied pigment around their hand, producing an unpainted image of their hand once the hand was removed. I will illustrate this technique in the planter project on page 69; in this case, you use masking tape to "mask off" a design, then apply paint around the mask. Removing the masking tape reveals the design.

The second variation is what's known as a repeating pattern stencil. This is a simple concept: instead of using one stencil to create one design, the stencil is used to create a part of the design. I will illustrate this technique in the tile project on page 25. Using squares of a repeating pattern to form a larger repeating pattern has been a tradition in tiles as well as in quilt block patterns.

DESIGNING YOUR OWN REPEATING PATTERN STENCIL

When designing a repeating tile pattern, start with a square piece of paper. Fold the paper so that the bottom right corner is touching the top left corner. The design needs to meet exactly along the side where the page edges meet (what was the bottom edge of the square paper and the left edge of the paper). Holding the folded paper up to a window or light source will help you see whether the design lines up.

Now, open up the paper so it is square again. Fold the paper the opposite way (so the bottom left-hand corner is touching the top right corner). Again, the design needs to line up along the edge where the top of the square and the right edge of the square meet. Before cutting the design into a stencil, photocopy and print it out eight times. Cut out the squares and set them up as you would tiles to ensure that all the edges line up.

○ Fold the paper corner to corner to see where the design will meet when it repeats.

○ Holding the folded paper up to the window will help insure your design will meet and repeat.

Step-by-Step: How to Make a Repeating Pattern

1. Draw an image in the center of a piece of paper. Take up as much space as needed, but do not let the drawing touch the edges of the paper (A).

2. When satisfied with the image, cut it into four quarters (B).

3. Take these four quarters and switch them each diagonally. The bottom right-hand quarter should now be the top left-hand quarter. The bottom left-hand quarter will now be the top right and so on (C). Tape these together.

4. In the center space created, add another drawing or any design element (D). This will make an indefinitely repeatable pattern in all directions.

5. To ensure the pattern is what was desired, scan the image and line it up in a photo-processing program to see the results before you cut a stencil (E).

A

B

C

D

E

Enlarging a Design

Using either a stencil template from this book or a custom design, the first step in creating a stencil involves enlarging the template to fit the size of the project. (Note: Not all templates need to be enlarged, and if that's the case, simply proceed to the next section on transferring the design.) There are two common techniques for enlarging stencils: one uses the poster printing option available in most home printers, and the other involves a projector.

PRINTER METHOD:

Enlarging a stencil using a word-processing program and a home office printer is simple, but the directions are different in each case. Basically, open the image in the word-processing document and format it to fit the entire page. Search "print as poster" in the help section of your program or in your printer (click "print," then "options" in most cases, and then "help"). It will print the image out on many sheets of paper that will need to be taped together to use. Be sure to organize the sheets of paper as they come out of the printer, and be ready with an adequately large working space and some tape to assemble the stencil.

PROJECTOR METHOD:

Projectors come in many sizes and prices ranges. Even the smallest commercially available projector can enlarge a small image to wall size and is all the average user needs. In a dark room, project the image onto the correctly sized stencil material that has been secured to the wall. Using a permanent marker, trace the projected image onto the stencil material.

○ Size the image to fit the projector.

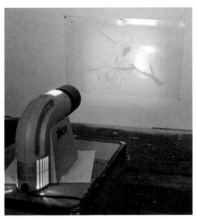
○ The darker the room, the easier it is to see the projected image.

○ The further back you move the projector, the larger the image becomes.

Transferring a Design

Once your template has been enlarged to the correct size (if needed), the next step involves transferring the design/template onto the stencil material. Stencil material can vary considerably depending on how large the stencil design is, how often the stencil will be used, and what medium will be used with the stencil.

By far, the easiest material to work with is clear plastic Mylar or acetate made specifically for stenciling (see Resources on page 141). Place the stencil template underneath the clear plastic and use a fine-point permanent marker to trace the design onto the stencil material. (When using a stencil burner with clear acetate, this step can be skipped altogether as described further along in this section.)

Other stencil materials that are not clear require the use of carbon paper to transfer the design. Readily available materials that make good stencils include the type of cardboard that cereal boxes are made from and manila folders. To use carbon paper (available at craft and office supply stores) for these types of stencil materials, place the carbon paper with the carbon side (darker side) down on the stencil material and then secure the stencil template with tape on top of the carbon paper. Use a ballpoint pen to firmly trace the template, causing the carbon to reproduce the image onto the stencil material.

○ This old wooden crate is soon to be art with the help of stencils.

Cutting or Burning a Stencil

There are two primary methods for cutting a stencil: with a craft or utility knife or with an electric stencil burner.

Craft knives (such as X-ACTO knives) should have a fine point and are used with a self-healing cutting mat. It is important to keep the blade sharp by replacing the blade often; the cutting of the knife will be smoother, and it is much safer. Craft knives can be used with any type of stencil cutting material, such as cardboard and acetate.

The stencil templates included in the back of this book are black and white. After you have chosen a design and transferred it onto the stencil material, all of the black areas need to be removed to make it a working stencil. When using a craft knife, do not secure the stencil to the cutting mat when cutting. It is often easier to move the stencil around rather than the craft knife. Holding the craft knife firmly and at a slight angle, use the very tip of the craft knife to remove all the black pieces from the stencil.

An electric stencil burner is like a wood-burning tool with a very sharp pointed end. It should be used over glass instead of a cutting mat. The metal tip gets very hot and easily burns the plastic as opposed to cutting it. This technique is much quicker than using a craft knife. Unlike a craft knife, the stencil burner easily moves in all directions, making curves a breeze. Also, very little pressure is needed, making it usable for people with hand or joint ailments. Stencil burners may be used with plastic-based stencil materials but not cardboard.

Another advantage to using a stencil burner is that you don't need to transfer the image to the stencil material if you use clear acetate or Mylar. Instead, place the stencil template underneath the glass work surface and then tape the clear stencil material on top of the glass. The image will be easy to see and trace with the stencil burner as you remove all the black sections.

Tips

- Use a stencil burner in a well-ventilated area.
- Use an emery board to keep the tip of the stencil burner clean and sharp.
- Purchase a glass work surface at a hardware store.

02.

PROJECTS TO PLAY WITH:

Inspiring Stencil Ideas

Scherenschnitte-Inspired Floor Tiles

D ramatically change the tone of any room with these easy to make and install self-adhesive vinyl floor tiles. Floor paint can be mixed in any imaginable color, providing far more options than commercially available floor coverings. The design for these floor tiles was inspired by Scherenschnitte, traditional German paper cutting.

Materials
- stencil template #1 on page 127, designed as a quarter-of-a-whole pattern
- clear stencil material and cutting tool
- self-adhesive vinyl tiles (follow manufacturer's directions to determine how many are needed for the space to be covered)
- medium-grit sandpaper
- foam paint roller for trim
- floor paint in two colors
- face mask
- repositionable spray adhesive
- masking tape

❖ VARIATIONS
If you have access to a kiln, you could make this project with ceramic clay tiles and ceramic paint or glaze. Many ceramic shops offer introduction classes or can fire stenciled tiles for a small fee.

INSTRUCTIONS

1 Prepare the Stencil

Prepare the stencil using template #1 on page 127 and the stencil cutting instructions on page 20. Cut or burn the stencil the same size as your tile. Use a clear stencil material for this project.

2 Prepare the Tile Surface

Using a medium-grit sandpaper, sand each tile just enough to rough up the surface and give it a "tooth" to hold the paint. Using a small foam trim roller, apply the base color to each tile (A). Follow the manufacturer's recommendations on drying times between coats.

3 Apply the Stencil to the Tile

Wearing a face mask and working in a well-ventilated area, spray a thin coat of repositionable adhesive on the back of the stencil. One application of spray adhesive will last for twenty to thirty stencil applications. Only reapply when the stencil is no longer adhering to the tile surface. The tiles all have the same pattern, but placed together they make up a larger repeating pattern. To make this larger repeating pattern work, it is important that the stencil be placed on each tile precisely the same way. After laying the stencil on the tile, use masking tape to help ensure consistent placement (B).

4 Paint the Stencil

Using the same type of soft foam trim roller and the second color of floor paint, firmly roll the paint over the stencil (C). Carefully peel the stencil off the tile (D). Repeat on as many tiles as needed.

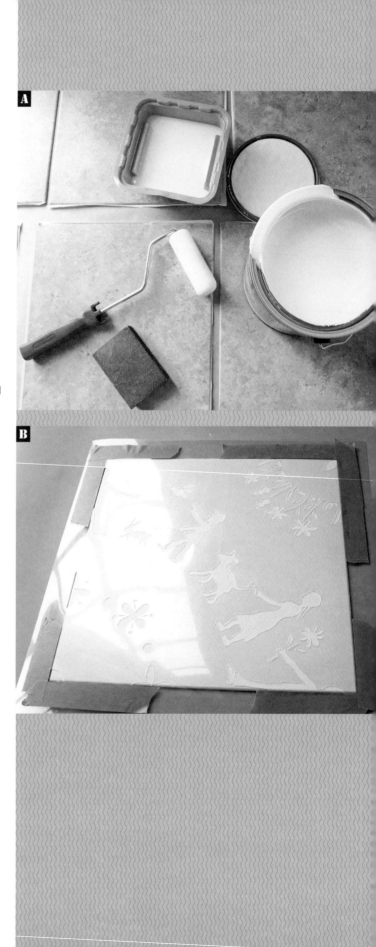

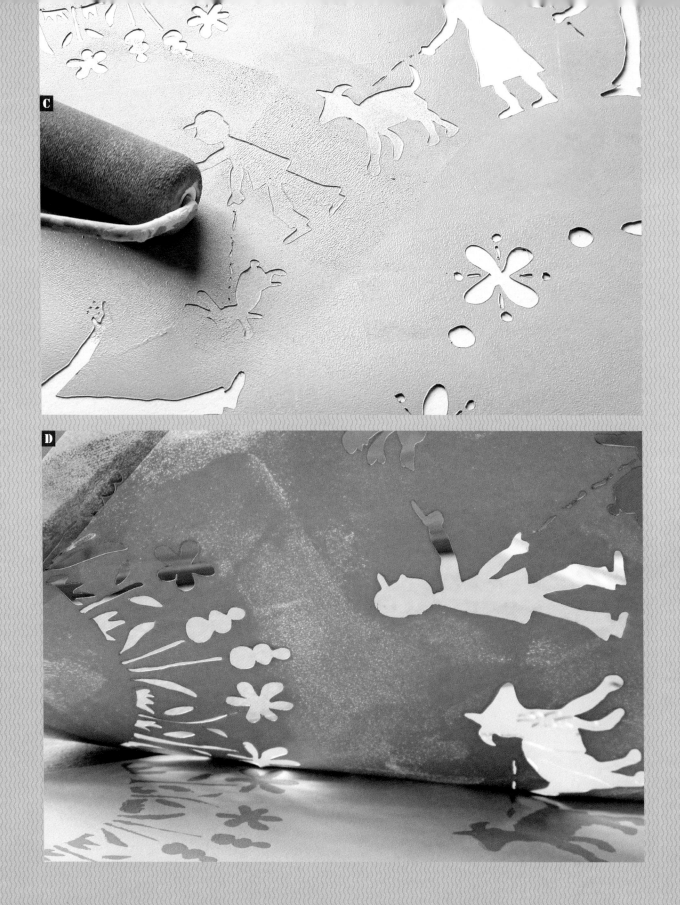

A Decorative and Challenging Puzzle

Don't let the simplicity of the design fool you; with 10,077,696 combination possibilities, this puzzle is far more challenging than it may appear. It's a fun conversation piece for a coffee table or an office, and even if the puzzle is never figured out, making patterns with the blocks is fun in itself.

Materials
) varnish
) paintbrush
) nine 3" (7.5 cm) wooden cubes
) two 11" (28 cm) square stencils
) pencil
) low-tack masking tape
) face mask
) repositionable spray adhesive
) spray paint in two colors

❋ **CONSIDERATIONS**
Making three different patterns or adding a third color may be tempting and may make the puzzle visually more interesting, but it will also make the puzzle exponentially less challenging.

❖ **VARIATIONS**
Any size wood cube will work, just be sure to cut your stencil 1 inch (2.5 cm) larger in diameter than the size of the combined cube square.

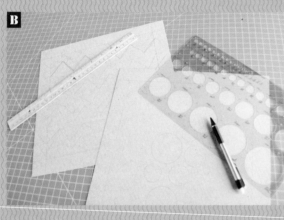

INSTRUCTIONS

1 Prepare the Wooden Cubes

Apply the varnish to all six sides of the cubes (A). This will need to be done in stages.

2 Cut the Stencils

Simple geometric designs work best. Cut out two 11-inch (28 cm) square pieces of stencil material (B). This could be a commercial stencil plastic or thin cardboard.

With a pencil (or fine-point permanent pen if using plastic), draw a 10-inch (25.4 cm) diameter square. Design the stencil in this box. Keep it simple. Make sure the design goes all to way to the pencil marks. Cut the stencil using the instructions on page 20 (C).

3 Set Up the Cubes

Set up the cubes three wide by three deep. Use low-tack masking tape around the sides to secure them together, leaving six surfaces facing up together to make one 9-inch (22.9 cm) diameter square surface (D).

4 Spray Paint the Stencil on the Cubes

Wearing a face mask and working in a well-ventilated area, lightly spray repositionable adhesive onto one side of the stencil and place the adhesive coated side down on the cubes as centered as possible. Press the stencil down securely onto the cubes. Spray the first color of spray paint over the stencil using a steady, consistent motion (E). Remove the stencil (F). Spray paint can remain tacky for up to 30 minutes depending on the humidity.

5 Reset the Cubes

Once the spray paint is completely dry, set up the cubes so that there are six blank surfaces on top again. Do not turn all the cubes to the left, or flip them all upside down. Choose the new "top" at random (G). Once again, use low-tack masking tape to secure the cubes together. Use the same stencil and the same color spray paint used last time, but this time instead of trying to center it, try to make the stencil a tad off center (F). Make sure the stencil will still go to the ends of the blocks, though. This will make the puzzle much more challenging because the sides will be almost the same, but not quite. Repeat a third time, trying to off-center the stencil in a slightly different way. Switch to the second stencil and a new spray paint color and repeat three more times. (See H for the finished set.)

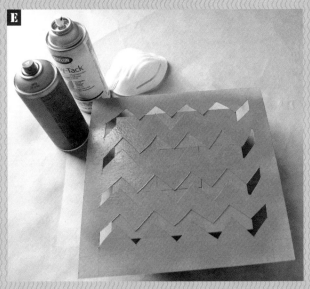

E

G

F

H

Stencils Love Decoupage:
Old Wood and Antique Letters

Spray paint adheres nicely and consistently to almost any surface. The shadowy quality of the spray paint through a stencil makes a nice effect in mixed-media projects made with found objects of varying textures. In this inspiring project, an antique wooden icebox decoupaged with antique correspondence finds new life as a coffee table.

Materials

- ❯ stencil template #2 on page 128
- ❯ face mask
- ❯ repositionable spray adhesive
- ❯ piece of furniture with at least one flat side
- ❯ metal scraps or alternatives to serve as paperweights
- ❯ flat black spray paint
- ❯ interesting paper for decoupage
- ❯ low-tack masking tape
- ❯ scissors
- ❯ decoupage medium

❖ VARIATIONS

Decorative craft paper, old maps, wrapping paper, and sheet music are just some of the types of paper that could be used in lieu of "paint" with a stencil in a similar project.

Paper can be ironed using an iron without steam on a high setting. In addition to smoothing out the paper, it can also set the ink, making the paper easier to use with water-based decoupage mediums.

Round heavy metal scraps from a local metal scrap yard serve as weights to help hold the stencil tight against the surface to be painted.

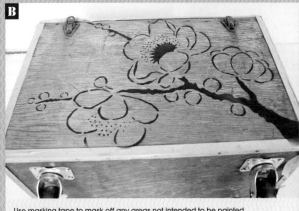

Use masking tape to mask off any areas not intended to be painted.

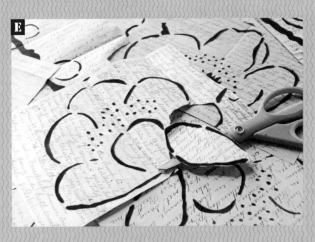

○ From the author's antique letter collection

INSTRUCTIONS

1 Prepare the Stencil
Prepare the stencil using template #2 on page 128 and the stencil cutting instructions on page 20.

2 Spray Paint the Guide
Wearing a face mask and working in a well-ventilated area, spray repositionable adhesive on the back of the prepared stencil. Next, place the stencil right side up on the surface to be decoupaged. For extra help securing the stencil, use metal objects to weight the stencil down and then spray paint the stencil onto it (A and B).

3 Make Letters into Petals
After the spray paint on the stencil has completely dried, flip the stencil over to the other side (which will be the sticky side due to the repositionable adhesive) and place the desired pieces of paper face down on separate petals. Secure the paper with low-tack masking tape (C).

Flip the stencil back to its front and spray paint using the same paint used for the guide. Wait for the spray paint to dry completely, flip over the stencil, and carefully remove the separate pieces of paper (D). Set them aside. Because the finished results will be far better if each touching petal is from a different decorative paper, this step will need to be repeated a few times (E).

4 Put It All Together
Using the image that was spray painted onto the furniture surface in step 2 as a guide, cut out and arrange the petals so that no two petals that are touching are cut from the same paper. Use a liberal amount of decoupage medium to secure the petals to the surface accordingly (F). When completely dry, coat the entire surface with another layer of decoupage medium.

A Simple Stencil for a Prettier Cake

Who doesn't like cake? And the prettier the cake, the better. Decorating cake with a pastry tube takes patience and practice. Using a simple stencil to decorate a cake is old-fashioned fun and can be custom cut for any occasion. Stencils can be used with powdered sugar or colored sugar on cake that is frosted or unfrosted. Small stencils can be made for cupcakes or cookies.

Materials
- pencil
- craft or waxed paper
- craft knife and self-healing mat
- toothpicks
- a plain cake
- powdered or colored sugar
- sifter
- pastry knife or spoon

✳ CONSIDERATIONS

Keep the design simple, and hence the cutting to a minimum, because this stencil will probably be used only once.

❖ VARIATIONS

Stencils work great on a frosted cake as well. Apply the stencil directly to the frosting and distribute the colored sugars with a spoon. Slowly remove the stencil; the frosting may stick, so use a pastry knife to smooth it down again.

Just a few gentle taps is all that is needed.

INSTRUCTIONS

1 Design and Cut the Stencil

Draw a simple stencil design with a pencil on craft or waxed paper in an area the same size as the cake. Using a craft knife on a self-healing mat, cut out the stencil (the areas that are cut out will be the design left on the cake) (A).

2 Apply the Stencil to the Cake

Use toothpicks to hold the stencil on the surface of the cooled, unfrosted cake (B). Make sure the cake has cooled completely or the paper might stick to the cake, ruining the effect.

3 "Paint" the Stencil with Sugar

Place the powdered sugar in a sifter (C). Using a pastry knife (or spoon), gently tap the side of the sifter over the stencil/cake, sending a light dusting of powdered sugar evenly over the entire surface (D). Carefully remove the toothpicks and bring the stencil up vertically and slowly so as not to spill any excess powdered sugar on the cake.

○ A stencil and a little powdered sugar can make a simple sheet cake look like an elegant bakery treat.

E

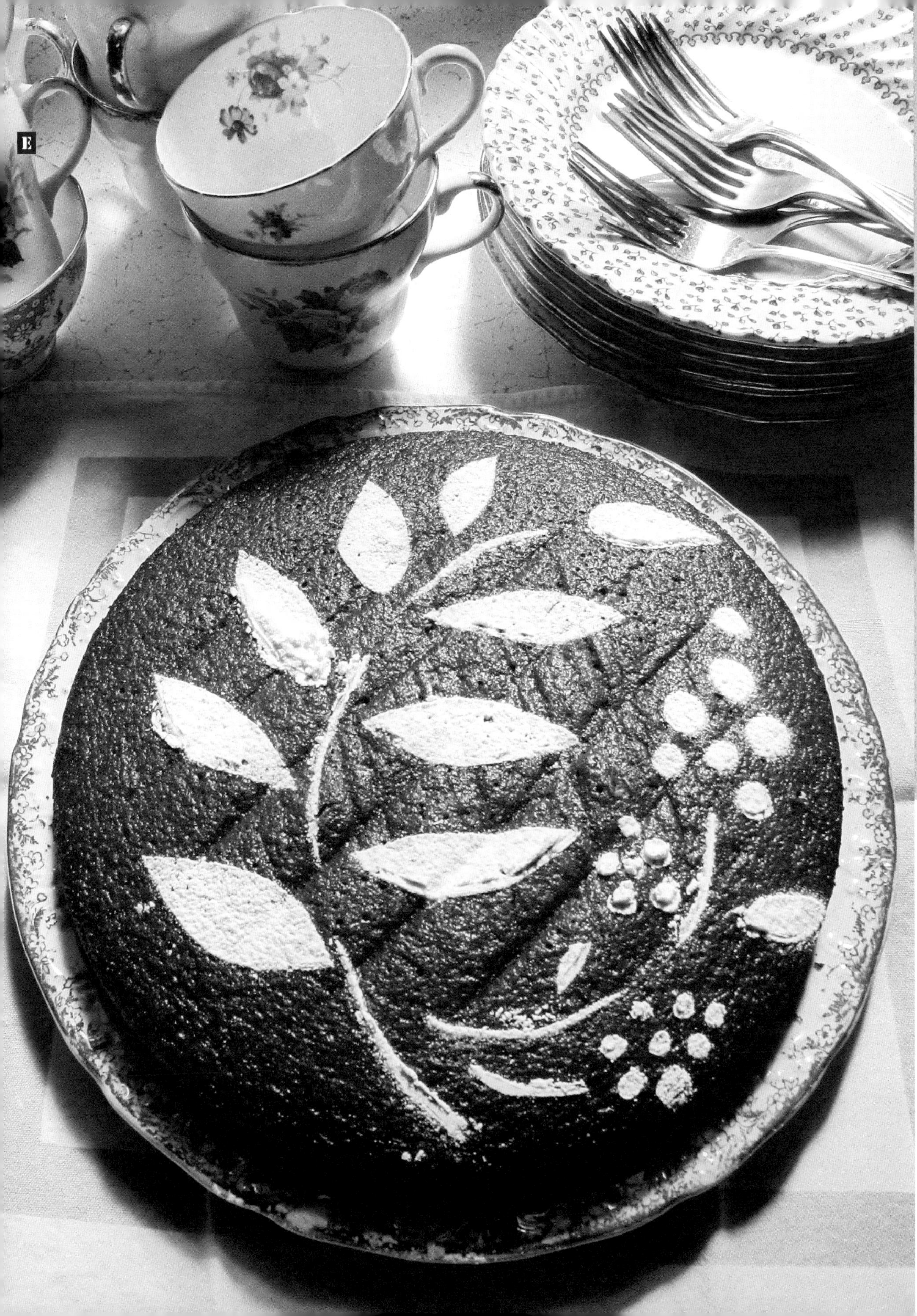

A Fun Floor Cloth

This durable floor covering is a deceptively simple and inexpensive project that can be made to match the color palette of any room. Canvas is the material more traditionally used for floor cloths. This project can be made with commercially available canvas made specifically for floor cloths. However, the commercial vinyl wallpaper is much more affordable, it is surprisingly durable, and the edges do not need to be finished in any way, unlike canvas.

Materials

- stencil template #3 on page 129
- commercial 54" (137.2 cm) vinyl wallpaper (see Resources)
- scissors
- T-square or long straightedge
- paint roller and roller tray
- latex floor paint in three colors
- masking tape, 2" (5 cm) or wider
- large spoon
- face mask
- repositionable spray adhesive
- scrap paper or cardboard for blocking overspray
- spray paint in two colors

❖ VARIATIONS

Research traditional rug motifs to find other designs for your floor cloth. Pulling out some basic elements from these complex designs and repeating them in a simple formation can result in a striking contemporary effect.

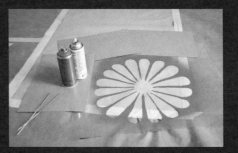

Wooden skewers may be used to hold the stencil on the surface when applying spray paint.

INSTRUCTIONS

1 Size and Cut the Stencils

Template #3 on page 129 has three stencils. Using the template and the instructions on pages 18 and 20, enlarge and then cut out the stencils.

2 Prepare the Surface

Cut the wallpaper to the desired size. To get squared corners, use a T-square (A). The "toothy" back of the vinyl wallpaper will be the work surface; it holds paint well. Use a paint roller to paint the entire surface with two coats of the background base color (B), drying in between.

3 Paint the Border

Using masking tape 2 inches (5 cm) wide or wider and a T-square (or straightedge), mask off the center (C). Press it down. Using a roller and a second color, paint the base color of the border (D) with two coats.

4 Add the Border Stencil

Plan out how to fill the border space with the leaf stencil. Wearing a face mask and working in a well-ventilated area, spray repositionable adhesive on one side of the leaf stencil and place it on the border (E). Using a roller

and the third color of paint, roll the paint over the stencil (F). Let dry and then roll a second coat. Move the stencil over to fill another space on the border. Flip it upside down or keep the pattern going in the same direction.

5 Add the Center Flowers

Mask off the completed border using scrap paper or cardboard before you work in the middle (G).

Use the large flower stencil first. Spray repositionable adhesive on the reverse side and place it in the center of the floor cloth.

Spray paint tends to send a fine mist out a long way, creating an "overspray." Use scrap paper to make a wide border around the flower stencil to block the overspray (H).

Use the first color of spray paint to spray in the flower. Let it dry and then move the stencil to another place in the center (I). It is okay if some of the petals reach out into the masked-off area of the border.

Continue to add flowers until the center is full (J).

Use the smallest stencil of template #3 and the second color of spray paint to finish the middle of the flowers (K). Remember to block the overspray (L).

Wall Art: A Pack of Sweet Shelter Dogs

As an art method, stencils are fantastic because the same stencil can be painted in a number of different ways. Three dog stencils can turn into a pack of nine (or more!) different dogs. This art project was inspired by my online search for just the right dog that needed a home. All three images came from shelters and rescue agencies attempting to find forever homes for these cute pooches. Any dog, cat, or pet photo can be used. This project would make a fantastic gift!

Materials
- stencil templates #4, #5, and #6 on pages 130-132
- 9 square art panels, wood or canvas
- matte acrylic craft paint in multiple colors for background
- paintbrushes
- face mask
- repositionable spray adhesive
- scrap paper or cardboard for blocking overspray
- matte black spray paint
- colored pencils (optional)

❖ VARIATIONS
You can use this technique for any pet portrait, and if you feel ambitious, you could even try it using your favorite humans as subjects.

A

Tip: Designing Your Own

- To design the stencils for this project, I took the photos I found online of dogs in shelters, made them black and white in photo-processing software, and then tweaked the brightness so that the images were light. I printed them out onto a standard-size sheet of typing paper and with a marker traced the strongest lines (keeping the rules of stencils from chapter 2 in mind). Use this method to find pictures of shelter dogs (or cats or rabbits) you think are art worthy.

INSTRUCTIONS

1 Size and Cut the Stencils

Larger stencils are much easier to cut, so depending on your skill level, art panels larger than 8 inches (20.3 cm) may be best. Size and cut the stencils so they are a little smaller than the panel size using the instructions on page 20.

2 Prepare the Panels and Spray the Stencil

Select a palette that will complement the colors of dogs to be painted. Use acrylic craft paint to add a solid color field to each panel surface. Allow to dry. Wearing a face mask and working in a well-ventilated area, spray repositionable adhesive on the back of one dog stencil. Lay the stencil on the panel. Use paper or cardboard to block the overspray. Spray the black paint onto the stencil

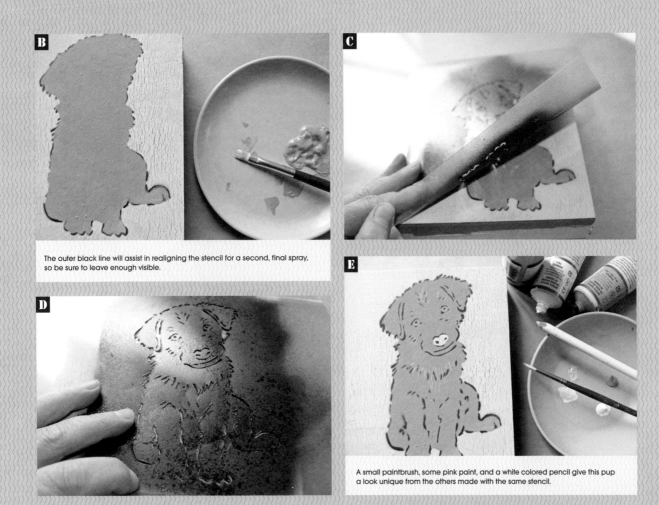

B The outer black line will assist in realigning the stencil for a second, final spray, so be sure to leave enough visible.

E A small paintbrush, some pink paint, and a white colored pencil give this pup a look unique from the others made with the same stencil.

on the panel. Position the same dog on a second panel of a different color. Try to place it in a way that is different from the placement of the first one and spray paint. Let the stencil dry completely. Spray repositionable adhesive on the reverse side (the side that now has spray paint on it) of the stencil. Place the stencil on a third panel, adhesive side down. This will make the third dog face in the opposite direction. Repeat this step with the second and third dog stencil for a total of nine panels (A).

3 Paint in the Puppies

Use matte acrylic craft paint to paint in each dog a different solid color; paint right over the stenciled design, but leave a good deal of the outer black spray paint line

so that the stencil can be repositioned correctly (B). Do not worry about details, such as coloring in their noses or giving the dogs spots, at this step.

4 Reapply the Stencil

Lay the corresponding dog stencil facing the appropriate way onto the colored-in dog. Use the outer black lines of the dog to align the stencil in the same exact position it was sprayed the first time (C). Apply another layer of matte black spray paint (D).

5 Add the Details

Use more acrylic craft paint and colored pencils to add details to make each dog special and unique (E).

Projects to Play With

Paper Dolls Please

ven modern children love paper dolls. They are even better when they are made by hand and even better than that with little helper hands. The dresses also make cute décor for a little girl's room when framed as art.

Materials
- stencil templates #7 and #8 on pages 133 and 134
- clear stencil material
- stencil burner
- face mask
- repositionable spray adhesive
- scrap paper or cardboard for blocking overspray
- flat black spray paint
- variety of fun paper (wallpaper samples pages, origami paper, printed scrapbooking paper, etc.)
- heavy craft paper (one being a skin color)
- craft paints (white plus other colors as desired)
- markers or colored pencils
- doily (optional, for slip)
- scissors

✹ CONSIDERATIONS
When making a batch of paper dolls for a child, do the spray painting in advance. Let the dolls air out for a few hours so all the fumes are gone. Print the clothes onto plain white paper and they will be like coloring book pages. Kids can use crayons, colored pencils, or watercolor paints to decorate their dolls and the dolls' clothes.

❖ VARIATIONS
The paper doll dresses hold infinite possibilities for design and color. Paint in three and frame them to match an interior design scheme or give as a baby shower or other gift. It is easy to make a bunch of "blanks" at once to save and paint in at a later date.

Using a variety of different papers can make one stencil seem like many.

A pink-colored pencil adds blush to her cheeks.

All sorts of mediums can be used to add details to the paper doll clothes.

The dolls and dresses are easier to paint and draw on before they are cut out.

Grace is coloring her doll's dress to match her own.

INSTRUCTIONS

1 Size and Cut the Stencils

Use the stencil templates #7 and #8 on pages 133 and 134, following the instructions on page 20 for using a stencil burner, and clear acetate or Mylar to enlarge and prepare the stencils. The doll should be at least 8 inches (20.3 cm) tall for cutting ease. Be sure to size the doll and the clothes at the same percentage or the clothes won't fit.

2 Spray Paint the Stencils on Paper

Gather together the doll stencil and the clothes stencils. Make sure you paint the clothes facing the same direction as the doll (or again, the clothes won't fit). Wearing a face mask and working in a well-ventilated area, spray repositionable adhesive on the back of the stencil (use spray adhesive lightly and sparingly with paper) and then apply the stencil to the different colors and patterns of paper for the clothes. Use paper or cardboard to block the overspray. Apply matte black spray paint to the stencil dress designs on the variety of papers (A).

Follow the same printing instructions for the doll as for the dresses. Use a skin-toned heavier stock paper for the paper doll. Use craft paints, markers, or colored pencils to add details (B). A doily makes a cute slip. Spray the doll stencil onto a paper doily and cut the slip out from that and then glue it to the doll.

3 Make the Dresses Pretty

Use white acrylic paint to paint in each of the "tags" that hold the clothes onto the doll. Use other acrylic paint, colored pencils, or markers to add details to the coats and dresses (C). It is easier to paint them in before you cut them out (D).

○ Shadow box frames highlight delightful little paper dresses.

Freezer Paper Stencil: Fabric for a Favorite Chair

Freezer paper stencils work great for fabric projects where a clean, sharp line is desired. They can only be used once, so they are best for projects where just one piece of very special fabric is needed. They are also unique in that the laws of stencil bridges can be (sort of) ignored. This project was inspired by a favorite chair that needed a new fabric cover, a desire to match said chair with a trunk decorated in antique handwritten letters, and a Simon and Garfunkel tune.

Materials
❯ fabric scissors
❯ iron
❯ fabric (at least 1 yard (91.4 cm), depending on size of chair seat)
❯ freezer paper
❯ masking tape
❯ yardstick
❯ pencil
❯ black marker
❯ craft knife and self-healing cutting mat
❯ old bath towel
❯ stipple brush
❯ black fabric paint
❯ iron

❖ **VARIATIONS:**
Snippets of handwriting from a letter written by a grandparent (or other loved one), photocopied, enlarged, and transferred to the freezer paper could be very sweet as well.

In addition to the pencil lines to keep the writing straight, angled lines are used throughout to keep the cursive handwriting slanting at a consistent angle.

If the handwritten piece has more than one "O", be sure to use a method to designate which "O" the center goes to. Writing LOOK on the piece with the correct "O" underlined is one way.

The wax coating on the freezer paper will cause it to stick securely to the fabric when ironed.

INSTRUCTIONS

1 Prepare the Fabric and Freezer Paper

Cut to size and iron a piece of fabric for the project. Standard-size freezer paper (sold in grocery stores) is smaller than a yard wide, but pieces can be taped together to fit.

2 Write Out the Words

Use a yardstick to pencil in horizontal guidelines on the unwaxed side of the freezer paper about 2 inches (5 cm) apart to keep the handwriting straight. Using a pencil, fill the entire space with writing. Use a black marker to make the lines of the letters thicker (A). Make bridges in and between letters if it can be done while maintaining the flow of the handwriting. (See page 12 for more information on designing a stencil and bridges.) An "A" or an "O" without a bridge here and there can be remedied further along in the project using the freezer paper stencil method.

3 Cut Out the Stencil

Place the freezer paper with the handwriting on a cutting mat and with a craft knife, cut out all the black marker lines that comprise the handwriting (B). When you come to a letter with a "hole" (like the middle of an "O"), cut the whole "O" out. Then cut the center piece out. Write on this center piece where it came from and set it aside.

4 Iron the Freezer Paper to the Fabric

Lay the freezer paper that has had all the words cut out onto the fabric (C). It is best to do this on one flat surface. Set the iron to a medium setting and iron the paper to the fabric.

5 Replace the Letter Centers

Take the letter centers that were set aside in step 3 and place them back where they go. Iron them down (D).

6 Stipple the Fabric Paint onto the Fabric

Use a stipple brush and black fabric paint to push paint through the stencil onto the fabric (E). Use an up and down motion and use pressure. Let dry and then give it a second coat. Let it dry overnight, and then peel off the freezer paper. Follow the manufacture's recommendations for setting the fabric paint.

D

Tips

- A handwriting pattern is the desired result; the actual words are really only important to the creator of the piece because very little, if any, will be readable in full sentences.

- Freezer paper cut to typing paper size can be put through a printer, but this requires patience due to the slippery nature of the freezer paper.

E

Custom Yardage: Fabric with a Repeating, Vintage-Style Pattern

or an interior design project (like decorative pillows—see the next project) where only a yard or two of fabric is needed, why not make it extra special with custom-designed fabric? The advantages to using spray paint over fabric paint are that it dries much quicker and there is no wait time between stencil applications. Fabric paint is generally more durable and can be used without ventilation concerns.

Materials
- clear stencil material and cutting tool
- iron
- 1 to 2 yards (91.4 to 182.8 cm) of cotton material in a light color
- masking tape
- fabric paint or spray paint
- stipple brush
- face mask (if using spray paint)
- scrap paper or cardboard for blocking overspray
- wooden skewers
- yardstick

❖ **VARIATIONS:**
Create striping using different elements. Rows of stars, tree shapes, pine cones, umbrellas, feathers, fish, or snowflakes would each create charming patterns.

○ Lines can be added to the design to change up the pattern.

INSTRUCTIONS

▌ Cut the Stencil

A stencil with a pattern that repeats in a line is a nice introduction to printing repeating patterns on fabric. Clear stencil material works best for this project because you will want to be able to see where your design line left off. Use the instructions on page 20 for cutting the stencil.

▌ Prepare the Fabric

Iron the fabric flat with an iron set on the cotton setting. Lay out as much of the fabric as there is space for on a flat surface. Be sure to protect the work surface because the paint may seep through the fabric. Position and tape the stencil at the bottom left corner of the fabric (A).

▌ Print the Stencil

If you are using fabric paint, apply the paint with a stipple brush in an up and down motion. Follow the manufacturer's recommendations for setting the fabric paint (often this involves ironing the fabric on both sides). If you are spray painting, work in a well-ventilated area and wear a face mask. When using spray paint, take care

to mask off the nearby fabric so that the overspray does not stain it. Use sticks (wooden skewers sold in grocery stores work great) to hold the stencil against the fabric as you spray. Repositionable spray adhesive used for this purpose in most projects in this book is inadvisable because it will leave the fabric sticky. A light touch on the spray paint can button is all that is needed when spray painting fabric.

Using clear stencil material in order to see where the pattern ended won't help very much if it is covered with spray paint. Put a piece of masking tape over the clear stencil material right where the design ends and begins (B). Pull it up to see where to line up the stencil and then replace it to spray the stencil. This tape may get very gooey, so replace it with a fresh piece of tape as needed.

Line up the next stencil application where the last one ended (C). Use a yardstick to keep the pattern aligned (D).

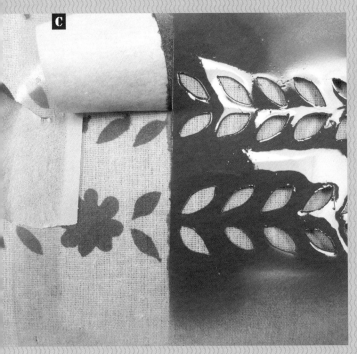

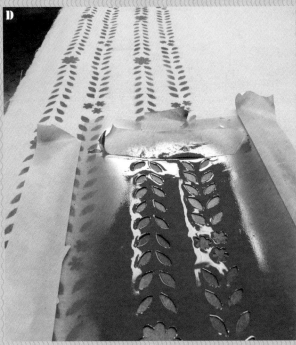

Tips

- The best fabric paints for use with stencils are the thicker ones that are more like acrylic paint, not the three-dimensional ones. Many brands of craft acrylics are formulated for use on fabric as well and are available in a wide range of colors.

- Choose paints made specifically for the fabric being used and follow the manufacturer's instructions for setting the pigment. Many become fast after ironing.

- When using fabric paint, masking off the other fabric is not necessary. A stipple brush is used to dab the paint onto the cloth through the stencil in an up and down motion.

Fabric Frames: A Pillow Gallery

intage bark cloth fabric and stenciled wool felt frames combine to make a fun and colorful gallery on large and decorative pillows. The fabric created in the last project serves as the "wallpaper" to pull it all together.

Materials
- stencil templates #9 and #10 on pages 135 and 136
- stencil material
- stencil burner
- face mask
- repositionable spray adhesive
- wool felt
- scrap paper or cardboard for blocking overspray
- black spray paint
- fabric scissors
- fabric for both the front and the back of the pillow (can be the same or different)
- T-square or other large straightedge
- vintage bark cloth or any scenic fabric
- white chalk pencil
- double-sided fabric fuse
- iron
- pins
- thread
- sewing machine
- pillow form
- hand-sewing needle

✸ CONSIDERATIONS
Choose pillow fabric that works with the frames created and plan how they should "hang" before cutting and sewing.

❖ VARIATIONS
Lots of different types of fabric could be used inside the frames. Try using an image from an old and well-loved T-shirt that has seen better days or a favorite photograph printed onto commercially available fabric made for home printers.

A stencil burner is best equipped to handle the small cuts used in this stencil template.

Real wool felt is much nicer than craft felt, comes in many beautiful colors, and is more readily available than it was in the past (see Resources).

A fabric frame.

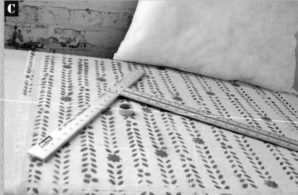

T-squares are helpful tools.

Move the frame around before you cut for good composition.

Fabric fuse works on a variety of materials.

INSTRUCTIONS

1. Make the Frames

The stencil templates provided on pages 135 and 136 were created by photographing actual frames. Use these stencil templates or use photographs of other frames to design a stencil. Size the stencil based on the size of the pictorial images from the fabric available using the instructions on page 18. Burn the stencil design into the stencil material using the instructions on page 20 (A).

Wearing a face mask and working in a well-ventilated area, spray a sparse amount of repositionable adhesive on the back of the stencil. Allow to dry. Lay the stencil on the felt. Use paper or cardboard to block the overspray. Use black spray paint to paint the image onto the felt. Cut out the frame with fabric scissors, inside the frame and around the outside edges (B).

2. Prepare the Pillow

For this project example, a 24-inch (61 cm) square pillow form was used. Because the pillow is fluffy, and taking a hem into consideration, two 27-inch (68.6 cm) squares of fabric are needed (the front and back pillow covers). Use a T-square to measure the pillow cover sides squarely (C).

3. Frame the "Art"

Lay the frame onto the decorative fabric and decide where the image looks best in the frame (D). Use a white chalk pencil to mark where to cut. Be sure to leave enough space around the image to secure it to the frame.

Trace the frame onto the double-sided fabric fuse and cut it out. Trace the fabric art image onto the fabric fuse as well. Use an iron to fuse the image to the pillow material first. Then place the frame on the art image and again use the iron to fuse it all together (E). Different brands of fabric fuse work differently, so follow the manufacturer's instructions.

4. Sew the Pillow Together

Pin the right sides of the front and back of the pillow cover together and sew almost all the way around (F). Leave enough space to turn the pillow cover right side out and to get the pillow form in. Finally, hand-sew the gap closed to finish the pillow.

F

Always test iron a sample of fabric before using the iron on the final project.

Avoid sewing altogether and use a premade pillow cover.

Tips

- Double-sided fabric fuse is a fun product that takes the sewing out of projects like this. Match the fabric fuse to the type of fabric used.

Classic Stencil Letters

There is a timeless quality to the font generated by the standard stencil letters readily available in hardware stores. After adding the name of your hometown or favorite place (real or imagined) to a worn item, it looks as if it could have been part of the object for years—an instant antique, custom made for a sentimental décor.

Materials
> stencil letters
> wooden box
> masking tape
> face mask
> flat white spray paint
> medium-grit sandpaper

❖ **VARIATIONS:**
Add lettering to kitchen chairs, kids' furniture, garden signs, gates, mail boxes, and more!

A flat white spray paint works best. White primer spray paint is a good alternative.

Remember that spray paint tends to overspray, so mask liberally.

INSTRUCTIONS

1 Line Up the Letters

Arrange the letters on the box or other object as desired (A). The letters can be separated out farther or overlapped to achieve the desired spacing. Don't feel limited by the letter spacing used by the manufacturer.

2 Mask and Spray Paint

Use masking tape to mask off everything but the letters (B). Wearing a face mask and working in a well-ventilated area, paint the stencils using a light touch and a sweeping motion with the spray paint can (C).

3 Sand for an Aged Look

Using medium-grit sandpaper, lightly sand the letters to the desired effect (D).

Reverse Stencil Planters

A reverse stencil uses a masking method to create an image outside the shapes masked off. In many ways, reverse stencils are easier because you do not have to worry about bridges and other stencil tricks. This planter gets an easy facelift with just a few steps and minimal materials.

Materials
- masking tape, thin and wide
- flowerpot
- craft knife and self-healing cutting mat
- round stickers
- face mask
- spray paint

❖ **VARIATIONS:**
Simple graphic patterns create powerful designs. For an alternate design, create horizontal rows of circles around the rim of your pot. Vary the spacing between rows for added interest. The advantage of reverse stencils is seeing your pattern in advance. If you don't like how it looks, just peel off the stickers and rearrange until you are happy with your design.

INSTRUCTIONS

1 Mask a Design

Use very thin masking tape to make the stems of flowers and grass on the flower pot. Masking tape this thin curves readily. Work spontaneously and let the stems overlap each other. Tape a few inches of the thicker masking tape to a cutting mat, use the craft knife to cut out leaf shapes (A), and then add them to the pot. Small circles are hard to cut this way, so use a variety of round stickers readily available in office stores to create flower parts and petals (B).

2 Spray Paint the Pot

Wearing a face mask and working in a well-ventilated area, spray paint the pot (C). Use a color that will contrast with the natural color of the pot for best results.

3 Reveal the Design

Let the spray paint dry completely. Peel away all the tape and stickers to reveal the design underneath (D).

Lace Stationery

here are a lot of readily available objects that, while not made to be stencils, can be used as such. Paper doilies and lace are just two examples. In this project they are used to make romantic stationery.

Materials
- paper doilies
- face mask
- repositionable spray adhesive
- blank cards and envelopes
- paper or cardboard for work surface
- small paint roller
- acrylic paint

❖ VARIATIONS:

Fabric lace is also an instant stencil. When using fabric lace, spray the repositionable adhesive just as you did with the paper doily. However, the fabric will move around too much to leave a sharp image with a roller and acrylic paint. Spray paint works much better with fabric lace.

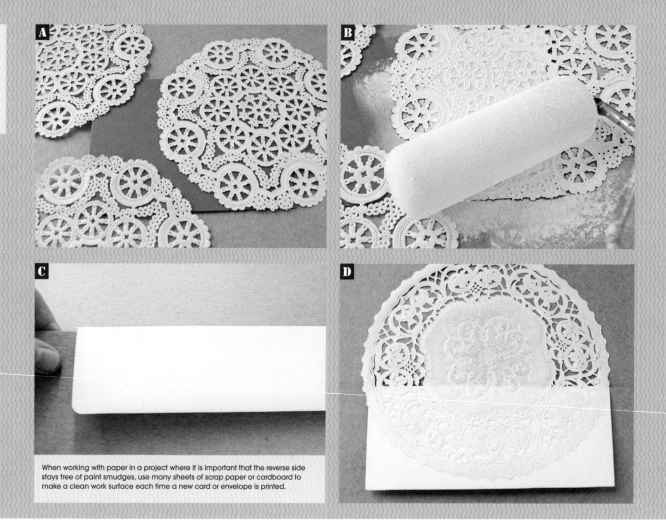

When working with paper in a project where it is important that the reverse side stays free of paint smudges, use many sheets of scrap paper or cardboard to make a clean work surface each time a new card or envelope is printed.

INSTRUCTIONS

1 Place the "Stencil" on the Card

Paper doilies are very thin and come in a stack that is tight together. When using them for their intended purpose (as doilies), it is sometimes difficult to separate them. When using paper doilies as a stencil, keeping a few stuck together will help them hold up better. Wearing a face mask and working in a well-ventilated area, spray a sparse amount of repositionable adhesive on one side of each doily or doily stack to be used. Let dry. Cover your work surface with scrap paper or cardboard. Place the doily on the front of the card and pat it down so that it is secure against the paper surface (A). Use a small paint roller and acrylic paint and roll over the card (B). Carefully lift the doily off. Use a new doily for each card.

2 Make Matching Envelopes

To make matching envelopes, place the envelope between two pieces of scrap paper or cardboard so that only the flap is exposed (C and D). Use the same technique to decorate the envelope flap (E).

⊙ Stacks of doilies

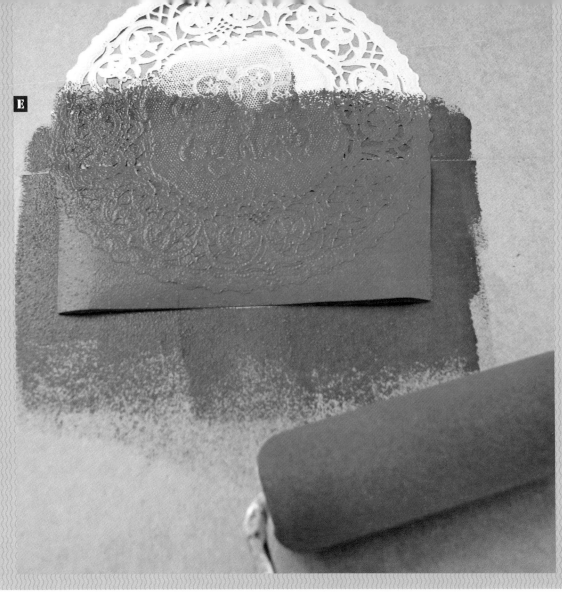

Faux Wood Inlay with Stencils

ood inlay is an intricate craft that requires a lot of tools and skills.
This faux wood inlay technique uses stencils for a fantastic result
that rivals the real thing.

Materials
> sandpaper
> wooden chair or other wooden object
> three distinct colors of gel wood stain
> paper towels, scrap cloth, or rag
> masking tape
> craft knife with many sharp blades
> freezer paper
> pencil
> face mask
> repositionable spray adhesive
> soft-bristled paintbrush

Multiple shades of stain create a lovely faux-inlay effect.

A

Firmly slicing a line into the wood surface with a craft knife makes the wood inlay look more real in two ways. It creates a very small gap where the stain gets caught up and doesn't bleed into the adjacent space. Also, it mimics wood inlay by giving the false impression that there is actually more than one piece of wood.

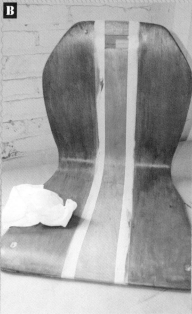

B

Gel wood stain soaks in quickly. Use a paper towel or rag and work fast to avoid an uneven finish.

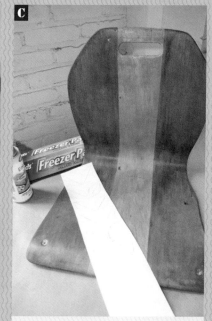

C

Freezer paper is employed as the stencil.

D

Be patient and cautious because a slip of the knife cannot be fixed. Sharp blades on the craft knife are a must. Change the blades often.

E

A "map" of the stencil on paper where each leaf section can be placed to get them back in the correct space later in the process is very helpful.

INSTRUCTIONS

1 Prepare the Surface

Sand the object to bare wood. Apply the lightest color of the stains with a paper towel and stain the entire surface. Mask off the area for the faux wood inlay design. Using a sharp craft knife, follow the outside edge of the tape and slice a line into the wood surface (A). Rub in a darker color of stain outside the faux wood inlay design area (B). After the stain has dried, remove the tape.

2 Prepare the Stencil

Cut a piece of freezer paper the size of the area intended for the faux inlay design (C). On the shiny side, draw the design in pencil. Simple geometric patterns work best. Wearing a face mask and working in a well-ventilated area, spray repositionable adhesive on the other side of the freezer paper and let it dry. Press the freezer paper with the design side facing up onto the surface of the chair.

3 Cut the Stencil and the Surface

Using a sharp craft knife, cut the stencil while it is adhered to the wood surface. Cut into the wood surface (D). Work slowly and with a firm hand.

4 Remove a Stencil Section

Remove all the stencil pieces needed to reveal the wood that is to receive the first stain color. The design pictured has three colors: the background color (the lightest) and leaves in two distinct stain colors. The bottom part of the leaves will all be the same stain color, so remove all the bottom leaf sections of freezer paper (E). These will be needed again, so set them aside.

5 Stain in the Stencil, Part 1

Now that all of the areas intended to get the second stain color have been exposed by removing part of the freezer paper stencil, the second stain color can be applied. Use a very soft, good-quality brush to stain in these areas (F). Two coats may be needed. Let this dry completely.

6 Stain in the Stencil, Part 2

When the stain on the first stencil area exposed is dry, replace the stencil pieces that you set aside (G). Now, remove the other stencil pieces to reveal the last areas to be stained. Add the third stain color (H). Let it dry and then remove all freezer paper.

Use a soft, high-quality brush to avoid brush marks.

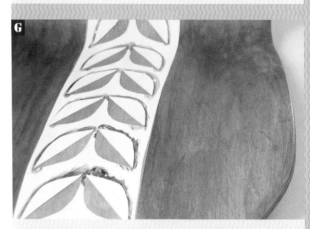

Replace the stencil pieces to cover the dry stain areas just commpleted.

Add the last stain color to the leaves.

Gig Poster

This gig poster for a couple of hardworking Minneapolis bands was inspired by typeset letterpress posters. Old-fashioned typeset letterpress posters often relied on many different fonts in one poster simply because there were only so many letters available in each font. This gave these posters a unique look and feel that can be replicated using fonts in your computer to make hand-cut stencils.

Materials
- computer with word-processing software and printer
- scissors
- poster paper
- small paintbrush
- white acrylic paint or correction fluid
- stencil material and stencil burner
- face mask
- repositionable spray adhesive
- small paint roller
- house paint in as many colors as desired
- stipple brush

❖ **VARIATIONS:**
It's fun to try different color combinations each time a new poster is printed. This technique could be applied to all manner of poster making: bake sales, rummage sales, school plays, or even fine art printmaking with typography.

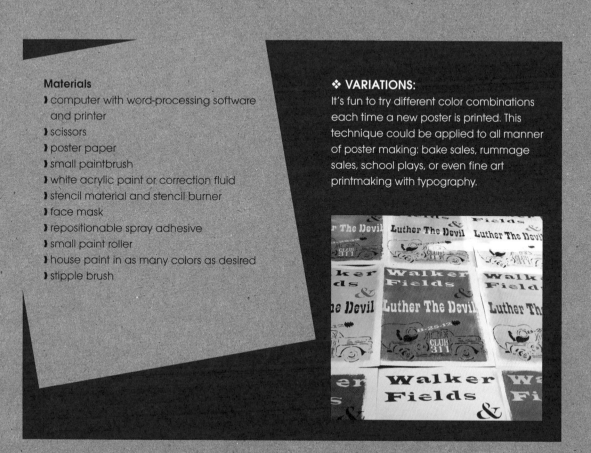

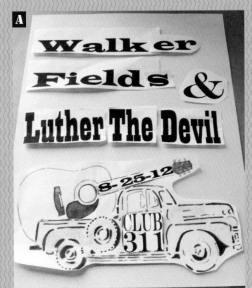

Not all type fonts are the same size at the same number given. For example, the top font was printed at 200 points, while the bottom font was printed at 140 points, even though they are the same height.

Any font can be made into a stencil-friendly font with a few bridges.

INSTRUCTIONS

1 Select, Print, and Lay Out the Font

In a word-processing program, type out all the information required for the poster. Change the fonts so that not all the lines of type are the same. Choose fonts that are simple and easy to read. The size of the poster paper to be used will determine how large to size and print the

words needed. Print out the type and cut and arrange the words on a poster to ensure all the information will fit (A).

2 Make the Letters Stencil-Friendly

Use a small paintbrush and some white paint (or correction fluid) to make bridges in any letters that contain an enclosed space (B).

3 Set the Type

In a real letterpress you would carefully set each letter, allowing the distance between each letter to be variable depending on the desired aesthetic. Do not depend on the spacing given to your letters by the computer program. Cut out each letter and place it in the poster space for a more authentic letterpress look (C).

4 Cut the Stencil

Letters and pictoral elements have many curves and detailed cuts, so it is highly recommended that a stencil burner and suitable stencil material be used for this project (D). Follow the instructions on page 20 to prepare and cut your stencil.

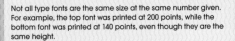

Tips

• In a word-processing program, the font size can be any size needed, not just the number sizes given. Highlight the letters to be sized and type the number in the font size box.

• Many stores that sell house paint have mistake or re-turned paint available at a steep discount. Some stores call this "oops" paint. Additionally, small jars of sample house paint contain enough paint to make dozens of posters at a minimal cost and can be mixed to any color desired.

The pictorial element of the poster is optional and should be simple and relate to the event. The truck and guitar image (by the author) alludes to the band's acoustic leanings.

Large letters are much easier to cut, and large posters are easier to read, so don't be afraid to go big.

House paint works well because it is thick, goes on well with a roller, and is waterproof (if you'll be hanging the poster outside).

Use a stipple brush for smaller areas where a different color is desired.

5 Add the Paint

Wearing a face mask and working in a well-ventilated area, spray repositionable adhesive on the back of the stencil and let dry completely. Place the stencil carefully onto the poster paper. Using a paint roller and house paint, roll paint over the letters (E). More than one color can be used; try changing it up for each font. Use a stipple brush in small areas where two different colors come close together (F). Carefully remove the stencil and make another.

Faux Braided Rag Rug

Braided rag rugs are a traditional craft made by braiding rags together and then sewing these braids into a flat surface. This project borrows on the design for a fun way to introduce custom colors to the floor of any room. The stencil for this project was created by taking a photograph of an actual braided rag rug. My intention in demonstrating how to make this particular project is to show that a stencil is most useful when it can be reused. With this technique, only one-fourth of the rug needs to be cut into a stencil rug.

Materials
- stencil template #11 on page 137
- stencil material and cutting tool
- scissors
- commercial 54" (137.2 cm) vinyl wallpaper (see Resources)
- latex house paint in four (or more) colors
- paint roller
- face mask
- repositionable spray adhesive
- scrap paper or cardboard for blocking overspray
- masking tape
- flat black spray paint
- medium paintbrush
- black marker

❖ **VARIATIONS:**
The faux braided rag rug could be painted directly onto the floor, or you could use commercially available floor cloth material.

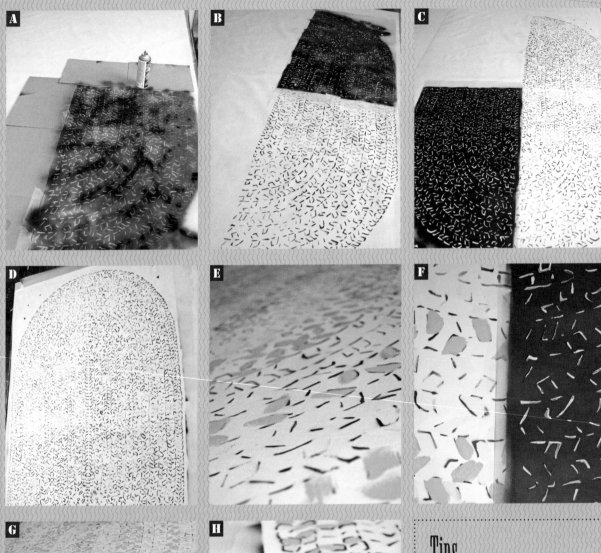

Tips

- The edges where the stencil meets will not line up perfectly due to the nature of the braid angle. It is not cheating to use a black marker and paint to help merge these areas together.

- Do not try to carefully stay in the lines and paint each little space in. In the time this would take, you could probably construct an actual braided rag rug.

INSTRUCTIONS

❶ Create the Stencil

Use the instructions on page 20 to prepare and cut the stencil.

❷ Prepare the Surface and Spray the Pattern

Cut a square piece of vinyl wallpaper large enough for the finished rag rug. Remember, the finished piece will be four times the size of the prepared stencil. The back of the vinyl wallpaper will be the work surface. It has a nice "tooth" that holds paint well. Use a paint roller and the lightest chosen paint color to paint the entire surface. Let dry completely.

Wearing a face mask and working in a well-ventilated area, spray repositionable adhesive on the back of the stencil and place the stencil on one corner of the painted wallpaper, curved side facing out. Use cardboard or paper and masking tape to mask off the areas where the rest of the rug will be. There is no need to mask off the rounded edge because this will be cut off and discarded later. Use the black spray paint to spray the first quarter of the stencil onto the surface (A).

A braid has a direction, and in a round braided rag rug it angles in the same way all the way around. To replicate this exactly, you would have to cut two stencils. Because the angle is not always too pronounced, this particular trait of a braided rag rug is ignored (or downplayed) in this project. The stencil will be sprayed four times, twice from each side. The side used for the first spray will be the same side needed for the corner diagonally opposite. Lining this one up next would be very difficult, so instead let the stencil dry completely, spray repositionable adhesive on the side previously spray painted, and use the stencil flipped to make the next quarter of the rug (B). It is not going to line up exactly (due to the braid angle issue previously mentioned). The outside edge (the rounded edge) of the rug should take priority in placement of the stencil for the next spray.

The next spray should be along the other inside edge of the first quarter spray, diagonally opposite the second spray (C). This is because that will be the direction the stencil will be facing after the last spray.

Finally, spray the fourth quarter (D).

❸ Paint in the Rags

An actual braid used to make real braided rag rugs is composed of three strands of rags. Every third angular

○ Do an Internet search for braided rag rugs to get a better idea of the patterns achieved using braids and simple blocks of colors.

polygon shape in a braided rag rug is the same color. Of course, fabric is often switched out, and so there are many variations. Keeping the every third rule in mind will help the finished product look more authentic. With a paintbrush, paint every third section using one color of paint (E).

❹ Replace the Black Lines with the Stencil

When all the color has been painted onto the rug, use the stencil and the same black spray paint again (F and G). Line up the stencil exactly the same way it was done the first time and follow the same order to spray the quarters again.

❺ Trim

Use scissors to cut the rug out (H). Follow the outside braided edge as opposed to making an exact oval for a more authentic look.

Retro Upcyled Tie

Old and ugly ties with outdated fabrics are easy to come by. Here is a fun project using such a tie, the freezer paper stencil method, and a reverse stencil technique.

Materials
- felt-tip marker
- paper
- carbon paper
- ballpoint pen
- freezer paper
- patterned tie
- masking tape
- scissors
- iron
- stipple paintbrush
- fabric paint or acrylic craft paint

Materials for retro tie making.

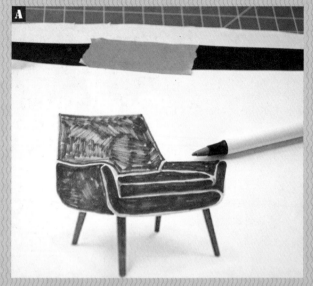

INSTRUCTIONS

1 Design and Transfer the Reverse Stencil

This project uses a reverse stencil, meaning that the area blocked off by the stencil will be the image that remains; everything around it will be the color of the paint used. Choose a simple image and, using a felt-tip marker and a piece of paper, turn that image into distinct shapes that do not touch each other (A). Notice how the photograph of a retro chair was turned into eleven shapes. Using carbon paper and a ballpoint pen, transfer the design to the unwaxed side of a piece of freezer paper (B).

2 Cut and Iron Design on the Tie

To avoid getting paint on the back of the tie, mask off the back with tape (C). At the seam joining the skinny back of the tie and the front fat part of the tie, place a piece of tape; this is where the paint will end.

Cut out each piece of the design and lay them on the tie as they were when they were together (D). It is helpful to have the original image with the pieces still together for reference. The shiny side of the freezer paper should be facing down, touching the tie. Use an iron set on medium to adhere the freezer paper pieces to the tie (E).

3 Add Paint

Use the stipple brush in an up and down motion to paint the entire front side of the tie (F). Let it dry completely and then remove the freezer paper pieces. Follow the manufacturer's recommendations for setting the fabric paint (often this involves ironing the fabric on both sides).

PROJECT

18.

Counted Cross-Stitch Stenciled Curtains

nspired by a traditional needlework motif, this counted cross-stitch design in red and black was popular with European peasants and early American immigrants. It makes a fun and contemporary pattern when enlarged to a different scale.

Materials
- graph paper
- plain curtains
- scissors
- clear stencil material
- T-square or yardstick
- red and black permanent markers
- stencil burner or craft knife and self-healing mat
- face mask
- repositionable spray adhesive
- stipple brush
- red and black fabric paint or craft paint
- masking tape
- iron

Materials for counted cross-stitch stencil.

A

B

C

D

E

1 2 3 4 5 6 7 8 9 10 11

F

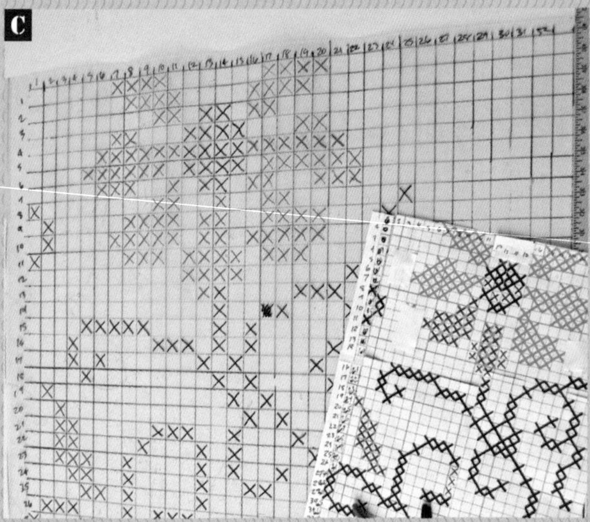

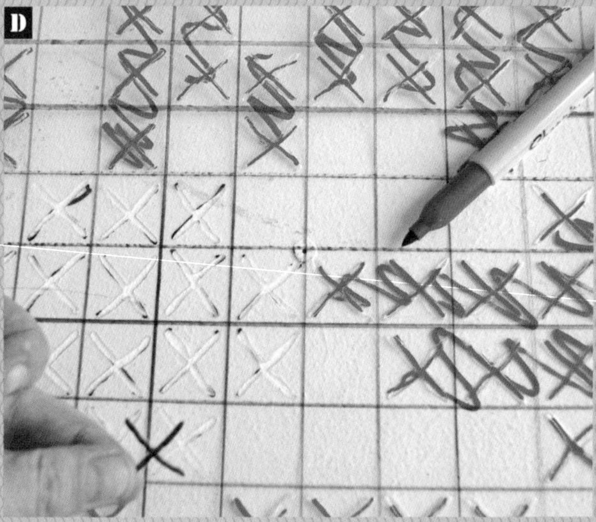

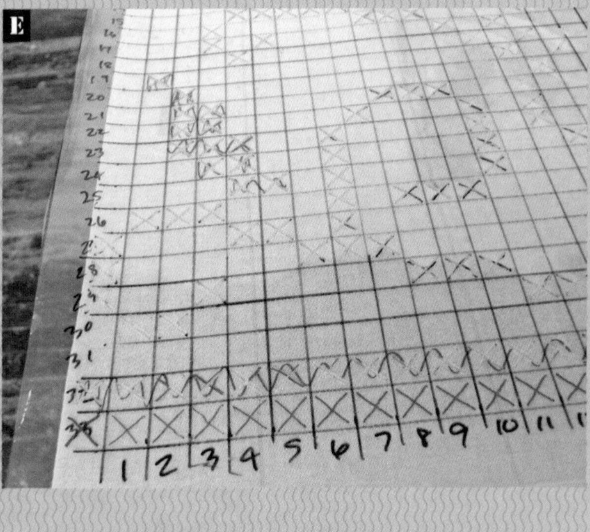

Use a thick fabric paint or acrylic craft paint.

INSTRUCTIONS

▪ Design the Pattern

There are so many cross-stitch embroidery patterns available. Books full of traditional motifs are also available in public libraries. Choose a simple pattern with one or two colors. Graph paper can be used to design your own motif or to modify a traditional design. Once you have chosen a design, number all the squares both vertically and horizontally, count the squares and then transfer the design onto your graph paper (A). It is called counted cross-stitch for a reason.

▪ Make the Stencil

Measure the curtains and determine the size of the motif. Cut a piece of stencil material a few inches larger than the motif. Using a T-square or yardstick, make a large graph with the same number of squares as the pattern (B). Number this the same way.

Using the design as a guide and permanent markers, place an "x" of the appropriate color in the correct square (C). Do not make the "x" go all the way to the corners of the square because this will cause spaces without bridges (see page 12 for more information about bridges) and the stencil will fall apart.

Using a stencil burner or a craft knife and self-healing mat, begin to cut out the crosses using the instructions on page 20. Remove the black ones first and then go over all the red crosses with the red marker (D). Do not remove them from the stencil as you go because once all the crosses have been cut and removed it will be difficult to tell which were red and which were black.

▪ Stencil the Curtain

Wearing a face mask and working in a well-ventilated area, spray the back of the stencil with a sparse amount of repositionable adhesive. Let it dry. Line up the edge of the stencil with the edge of the curtain (E).

Use a stipple brush and a firm up and down motion to work the paint into the crosses (F). More than one coat may be needed. Let the paint dry between coats.

Use masking tape to mask off separate colors when the crosses are in adjacent squares (G). When doing a repeating pattern, let the paint dry completely before moving the stencil over to the next section of curtain (H and I). Follow the manufacture's recommendations for setting the fabric paint (often this involves ironing the fabric on both sides).

Dancing in the Rain Shower Curtain

urning a sketch or doodle into a repeating pattern is easy with this low-tech method. A repeating pattern of geese and lovers dancing in the rain on a shower curtain makes for joyful bathroom décor.

Materials
) stencil template #12 on page 138
) clear stencil material and cutting tool
) plain vinyl shower curtain
) masking tape
) face mask
) repositionable spray adhesive
) scrap paper or cardboard for blocking overspray
) scrap metal pieces or alternative to serve as paperweights
) spray paint (look for spray paint made for plastic)

Materials for Dancing in the Rain Shower Curtain.

Scrap metal pieces are heavy and weight down the cardboard protecting the areas outside the stencil from overspray.

INSTRUCTIONS

1 Prepare the Stencil

Create the stencil using the instructions on page 16.

2 Stencil the Image onto the Shower Curtain

Lay the shower curtain out flat. It may help to hang it for a few days ahead of time to get out any wrinkles because it cannot be ironed. It will be important to line up the stencil edges exactly each time it is sprayed, so use masking tape to solidify the edge lines (A). Wearing a face mask and working in a well-ventilated area, spray the back of the stencil with repositionable adhesive and allow it to dry.

Place the stencil in a top corner for the first spray; stretch the vinyl shower curtain material out under the stencil to remove any wrinkles. Remember, spray paint gives off a lot of overspray, so protect the areas around the stencil with masking tape, scrap paper, or cardboard (B). Weight down the scrap paper with metal weights. Spray paint the first stencil.

It will be important to see the edge of the stencil each time it is sprayed for proper alignment. Spray paint will cover this line up. Add an extra piece of masking tape along the stencil edge to mask the line each time (C).

Use additional masking tape to keep the edges clean and easy to align. Replace it as needed.

Elements of the stencil can be masked off and painted a different color here and there to add an element of surprise to the repeating pattern.

3 Line Up the Stencil Edges for Subsequent Sprays

Wait for the spray paint from the first spray to dry. Line up the stencil so the edges are touching exactly. Peel back the tape used to mask the edge to ensure they are lined up correctly (D). After the second spray, the pattern will start to reveal itself (E).

Continue the pattern vertically, lining up the side edges. When the end of the shower curtain is reached, line up the stencil using the top and bottom edges to make the full pattern (F).

If there is space left at the bottom of the shower curtain that will not support the full design element, consider adding a border pattern (G).

Custom Wallpaper

A simple, vertically repeating pattern enlarged onto paintable wallpaper can be added to an entire wall like traditional wallpaper or used as a large piece of wall art.

Materials

- stencil template #13 on page 139 or custom-made stencil
- stencil material and cutting tool
- paintable wallpaper (see Resources)
- paint roller made for plaster
- house paint in three colors
- face mask
- repositionable spray adhesive
- masking tape
- scrap paper or cardboard for blocking overspray
- flat black spray paint
- paintbrushes

❖ VARIATIONS:
Frame just one stencil frame to make a graphic piece of wall art.

INSTRUCTIONS

1 Prepare the Stencil and Surface

Using the instructions on page 20, prepare the stencil. Enlarge the stencil to match the width of the wallpaper and cut it out.

Paintable wallpaper is highly textured (A); use a paint roller made for plaster for better paint coverage. Use the roller to paint the background color onto as much wallpaper as needed to fill the desired wall space (B). Do this on a large flat surface.

2 Spray the Outline Stencil

Wearing a face mask and working in a well-ventilated area, spray the back of the stencil with repositionable adhesive and allow it to dry. Place the stencil on the bottom edge of the painted (and dry) wallpaper. Remember to protect the areas around the stencil from overspray with masking tape, scrap paper, or cardboard. Spray paint the stencil onto the wallpaper (C).

Use masking tape to mask off the overlap where the bottom of one stencil spray meets up with the top of the next stencil spray for a seamless vertical design (D).

Wait for the spray paint to dry and then lay the stencil down again above the first sprayed image (E). Mask off any overlapping areas and spray again. Repeat this until the wallpaper section is full.

When moving on to the next section of wallpaper, start the stencil in a different place so that each section of wallpaper is not exactly the same (F).

3 Paint the Design

For this step, think of the wallpaper as a giant coloring book page and, using house paint and a paintbrush, color it all in, staying in the lines (G). Leave the outside edges of the black lines for alignment purposes in the next step.

When it has all been painted in and the paint has completely dried, place the stencil back onto the wallpaper. Use the outside black lines to lay the stencil in the exact place it was for the first spray on each section and spray again (H).

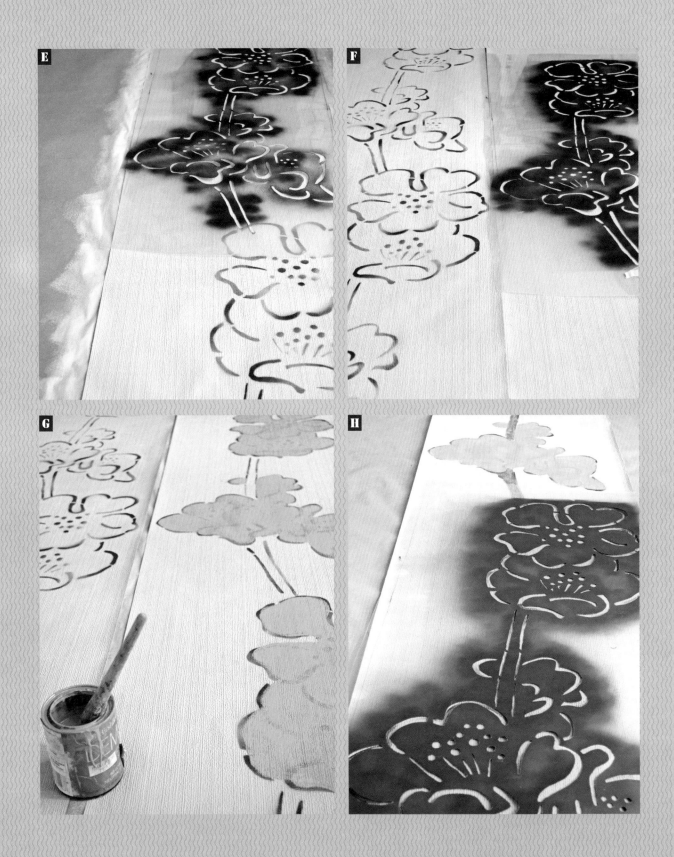

03.

Influential Contemporary Artists Who Use Stencils

Artist:

Rachel Breen.

"My art responds to life's fragile balance. I develop forms for these explorations by deconstructing sewing and its traditional purposes. Sewing is common across cultures, connecting materials for protection, decoration, and comfort. It reconnects what's been broken or torn—it's an act of making something whole again, or new for the first time. The very act of sewing suggests possibility.

"My work disrupts and subverts these purposes. I puncture the paper with thousands of holes from an unthreaded sewing machine that collectively describe personal and societal yearnings for cohesion and attachment. Lacking thread, the goals of repair, protection, and comfort are possible but never certain. My marks express a deeper desire for connection.

"The sewn papers also serve as stencils in my creative process. Through the holes of these stencils, I shake powdered charcoal onto paper or walls—a process called 'pouncing'—to create reverse-image drawings. When installed directly on the wall, the works appear delicate, fragile and temporary—a visual expression of our uncertain world.

"I hope to raise questions with my work, but am suspicious of easy answers. The holes created from an unthreaded needle look familiar but are difficult to identify. The work could appear as either falling apart or in the process of being put back together. In the end, the work suggests that merely having the tools to fix what is broken doesn't guarantee repair."

– Rachel Breen

TOP. *Let's Not Leave It to Chance*, 2011
Charcoal on wall, 18' x 35' (5.5 x 10.7 m)

BOTTOM. *Let's Not Leave It to Chance*, detail

TOP RIGHT. *Local Topography*, 2010
Charcoal on glass and internal window box, 3' x 4' (91.4 x 122 cm)

BOTTOM RIGHT. *Local Topography*, detail

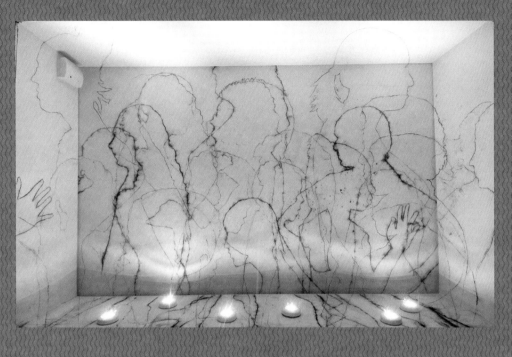

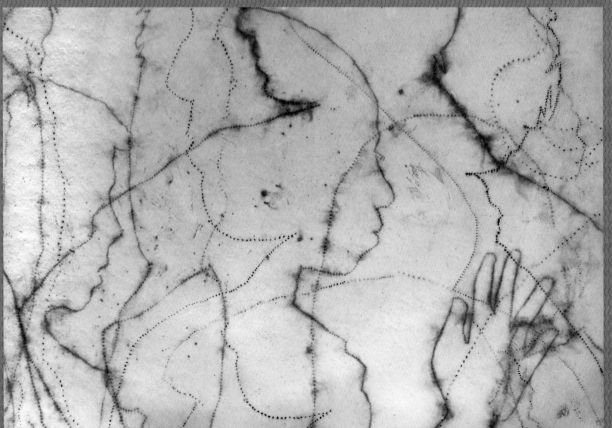

Artist:

Broken Crow.

Broken Crow is a stencil-based artistic collaboration between Mike Fitzsimmons and John Grider. The two artists began creating and showing art together in 2003. Since then, Broken Crow has attained global recognition for their pioneering use of large-scale stencils in the increasingly established arena of street art.

Through painting, Broken Crow seeks to reintroduce wild animals back into the urban habitats that we humans live in, writing their own mythology as they go. Broken Crow's aggressive style of painting, combined with their hyper-detailed stencils, is both playful and sophisticated. Their art features various animals and anthropomorphic humanoids in crazy colors and, of course, extraordinarily large size.

The effects of their efforts live somewhere in the vast gray area between street art and public art. As such, Broken Crow has contributed to countless exhibitions. To date, they have painted 120 murals around the world. Their mural art can be seen in Minneapolis, St. Paul, Duluth, Milwaukee, Chicago, Baltimore, Reno, Nashville, Austin, Dallas, Albany, New York, Paris, Mexico, London, and Africa.

TOP. *Ibex*, 2010
Hutchinson, MN

BOTTOM. *Elk*, 2011
Albany, NY
Photo Credit: Sebastien Barre (barre.me)

TOP RIGHT. *Lions*, 2011
Mexico City, Mexico

BOTTOM RIGHT. *Owls*, 2010
Minneapolis, MN

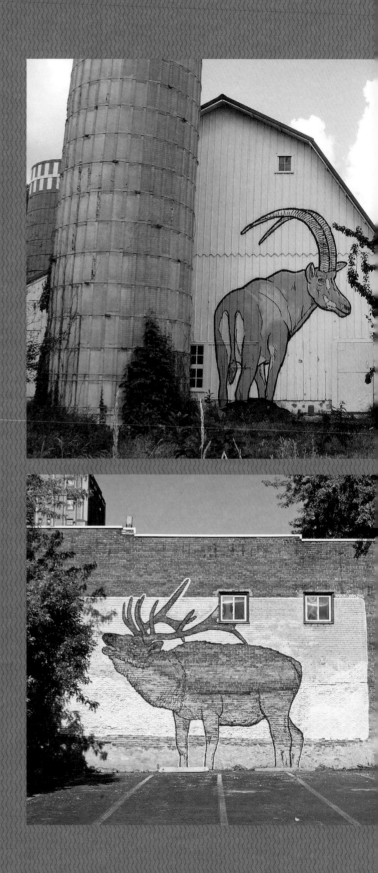

Artist:
Matt Dixon (aka M-ONE).

"Constant exploration of, and experimentation with, the medium of stenciled artwork has led me to turn my back on the use of stencils as a tool for tight graphic pieces, embracing instead the loose nature of the spray paint, often choosing as well to use the rather more random outcomes of working wet-on-wet, using water and white spirit, in order to achieve the desired results. Further elements, recently including rusting powder, are also used and, again, often left to their own devices so that the random nature of the process will add to the finished piece. The loose work, the essence of the piece, is then brought together by the judicious use of, usually, just two layers of cut stencils, comprising the black and white areas, which serve to add definition through line, shadow, accentuation, and highlight. The relative simplicity of using only two layers of stencils offers the opportunity for the identical reusable matrix to be used to explore different methods to achieve variable, and often widely differing, results within the context of the same image." – Matt Dixon

TOP. *Citroen H,*
Two-layer stencil, spray paint, and rust powder on reclaimed pallet wood, 19 2/3" x 23 2/3" (50 x 60 cm)

TOP RIGHT. *Tatty Kombi,*
Two-layer stencil, spray paint, and mixed media on canvas, 16 1/2" x 23 2/3" (42 x 60 cm)

BOTTOM LEFT. *Hummingbird,*
Three-layer stencil and mixed media on canvas, 15 3/4" x 23 2/3" (40 x 60 cm)

BOTTOM RIGHT. *Orange and Rust,* detail,
Three-layer stencil, spray paint, and mixed media on rusted canvas, 30 3/4" x 24" (78 x 61 cm)

Artist:

Christian Guemy / C215.

Christian Guémy, also known as C215, is a Parisian street artist focused on stencil graffiti. His striking portraits of local people, children, and especially his daughter Nina, are expressive and distinctive in style. With his subjects always portrayed as proud and dignified, his images communicate on a universal level and draw attention to those that society has forgotten about. His elaborate stencils—if outside a gallery—appear in the streets of various cities all over the globe, such as New Delhi, London, Istanbul, Fes, Rome, Barcelona, and Paris. C215's favorite topic is portraits because faces have a universal message that everybody, no matter who, will understand and be moved by. As C215 says, "In the end, behind the portraits, the question is always freedom and dignity in the face of a capitalist daily life system."

TOP LEFT. *Casablanca*, 2009 left

BOTTOM LEFT. *Brooklyn*, 2008

TOP RIGHT. *Morocco*, 2010

BOTTOM RIGHT. *Paris*, 2011

Artist:

Berry Holz.

Berry Holz grew up in Norseland, outside of St. Peter, Minnesota. She studied art history and interior design at the University of Minnesota. A self-taught artist, she turned her interest to acrylic and collage a few years ago. That way of making things led, through trial and error, to the process she really likes and works in now—a low-tech reverse stencil method done with spray paint and layered positive-image stencils. In 2011, she did a series of paintings for an in-patient psychiatric clinic, was featured in a small magazine, and illustrated a line of children's sticker play sets for Magnetic Poetry.

"The way things come out isn't always the way you intended them to—you don't get to control a lot of what you might really want to, either on a small personal scale or on a global one. I plan my paintings fairly carefully, then use masks and color to make them. I know what I'm after, but due to the method there's always an element of surprise when I peel the layers off at the end. Balancing color and subject matter (no matter what the subject is) to result in something that is easy to look at—a way to give myself or someone else a break—is what I'm hoping for." – Berry Holz

TOP. *Raccoon*, 2011
Spray paint on hardboard, 36" x 24"
(91.4 x 61 cm)

MIDDLE. *Winter Spring Summer Fall*, 2011
Spray paint on hardboard, 24" x 48"
(61 x 122 cm)

BOTTOM. *Fall Fox*, 2010
Spray paint on hardboard, 12" x 36"
(30.5 x 91.4 cm)

FAR RIGHT. *Spider Monkey*, 2010
Spray paint on hardboard, 18" x 24"
(45.7 x 61 cm)

Artist:

Megan Hunter.

"I am an artist who primarily works as a printmaker. I was born in Melbourne, Australia; I worked in the graphics industry before I went on to study printmaking and painting. I have been printmaking, making art, and showing my work ever since. I now live and work in Umbria, Italy.

"I am passionate about all art forms but love the many different effects one can achieve with the numerous techniques offered by the practice of printmaking—from the crayoned, soft line of a lithograph and the unparalleled rich tones of a mezzotint to the crisp etched lines, bold color, and exciting possibilities of serigraphy.

"The nature of printmaking lends itself to the multiple—multiples of the image to multiples of layers; it is mark-making that can etch an image with time or memories. It is a process that never truly reveals itself until you peel the paper back from the printed surface. Occasionally, it's a process that's discouraging, sometimes it's a wonderful surprise, but always it's enthralling and a challenge.

"My subject matter is relatively broad. I respond to the environment and time in which I am living as well as any issue that strikes a strong chord, such as a media report or a political decision I feel strongly about—anything from the destruction of old buildings in my city to an environmental concern, but generally my art tends to relate to location/environment, time, and political and social issues." – Megan Hunter

BELOW. *Lago Trasimeno Study 1*, 2012
Five-color stencil roll-up on an old etching plate, printed on Magnani paper, 10" x 15 ¾" (25.5 x 40 cm)

TOP RIGHT. *Trasimeno Lake Study-Winter*, 2012
Four-color stencil roll-up on an old etching plate, printed on Magnani paper, 9 ½" x 22 ⅞" (24 x 58 cm)

BOTTOM RIGHT. *Nylex-3 am*, 2006
Copper etching with stenciled color roll-up, printed on Somerset paper, 26.3" x 37.8" (67 x 96 cm)

Artist:
Liz Miller.

Liz Miller received her B.F.A. from the Rhode Island School of Design and her M.F.A. from the University of Minnesota. Miller's large-scale, mixed-media installations and works on paper have been featured in solo and group exhibitions regionally, nationally, and internationally.

"My mixed-media installations recontextualize simplified shapes, signs, and symbols from disparate historical and contemporary imagery to create abstract fictions. Existing forms from a multitude of sources are co-opted, altered, and spliced to adopt hybrid identities. Through the process of appropriation and subsequent recombination, I create an encyclopedia of simple, large-scale stencils during the preliminary phase of each project. The stencils form the backbone of the project, providing the architectural blueprint for the many parts that comprise a finished installation.

"Shapes lose their real-world connotations and take on fictitious roles. Forged relationships between benign and malignant forms confuse the original implications of each while revealing the precariousness of perception and how easily it can be tampered with. Recent projects pit Baroque and Gothic pattern and ornament against forms derived from armor and weaponry. Seemingly oppositional pairings create duplicitous environments where conflicting messages are conveyed. The use of felt, foam, and other tactile materials further complicates questions of source, masking the identity of forms while allowing them to inhabit both sculptural and two-dimensional space." – Liz Miller

BELOW LEFT. *Picturesque Evacuation Ploy*, 2011
Redux Contemporary Art Center, Charleston, SC
Stiffened felt and other mixed media, dimensions variable
Photo credit: Shannon Di

BELOW RIGHT. *Preposterous Cavalcade*, 2011
Coe College, Cedar Rapids, IA
Stiffened felt and other mixed media, dimensions variable

TOP RIGHT. *Ornamental Invasion*, 2011
Minneapolis Institute of Arts, Minneapolis, MN
Stiffened felt and other mixed media, dimensions variable
Photo credit: Amanda Hankerson

BOTTOM RIGHT. *Illusive Insurgency*, 2011
1708 Gallery, Richmond, VA
Stiffened felt and other mixed media, dimensions variable
Photo credit: Harrison Moenich

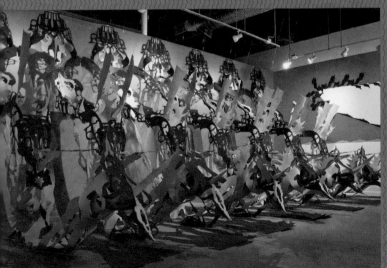

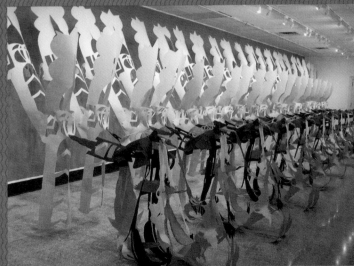

Artist:

Amy Rice.

Amy Rice is an artist based in Minneapolis, Minnesota. She has shown her work in galleries throughout the United States, Canada, the United Kingdom, and recently China. She is the author of this book.

"For the past ten years I have used nontraditional print-making methods—including hand-cut stencils and a Japanese screen-printing toy called a Gocco printer—as a starting point for original mixed-media pieces. I use spray paint, acrylics, gouache, and inks and print on antique papers. My surfaces have also included 100-year-old cedar shingles, barn boards, rusty metal, wooden and metal boxes, and wooden panels.

"I am most satisfied when I can make a tangible or visceral connection between the materials used and the image rendered. My work is deeply layered, often both literally and figuratively. My imagery—nostalgic and wistful—is largely biographical and reflective of my pensive nature." – Amy Rice

TOP. *Dear Elizabeth*, 2010
Spray paint, hand-cut stencil, and gouache on letter from 1938, 8" x 11" (20.3 x 27.9 cm)

BOTTOM. *It's a Closed System / The First Day*, 2010
Spray paint, hand-cut stencils, acrylics, inks, gouache, and Gocco prints on antique journal pages, antique letters, antique maps, paper, and paper lace, 16" x 20" (40.6 x 50.8 cm)

TOP RIGHT. *It's a Closed System / I Would Know You Anywhere*, 2010
Spray paint, hand-cut stencils, acrylics, ink, gouache, and Gocco prints on antique journal pages, antique envelopes, antique maps, paper, and paper lace, 20" x 16" (50.8 x 40.6 cm)

BOTTOM RIGHT. *Swan River 4-H Club circa 1948*, 2011
Spray paint, acrylic, and ink on wood, 42" x 24" (106.7 x 61 cm)

Artist:

Susan Rodriguez.

"Ceramica Botanica is my shop of hand-built functional pottery. My pottery is characterized by its bright colors and joyous, pattern-loaded surfaces. All the ceramic pieces are made by me from start to finish in my San Antonio, Texas, studio. The pottery I make is to be used every day—serving bowls, plates, and platters to be picked up, held, passed around the table, and filled with your wonderful culinary creations. Each piece is a one of a kind, handmade, and unique. I start by hand building with thin slabs of clay, creating pieces with clean, simple lines. Then the fun begins: mixing and playing with intricate patterns and joyous colors that will cover the tops as well as the undersides of each plate or bowl. I get crisp, bold patterns by hand cutting paper stencils and gingerly applying them to fit the piece. I create my own color palette by mixing ceramic stains with the clay body in small batches. The effect is bright colors with a rich, earthy tone and subtle variations in shades from piece to piece.

"Botanical forms fascinate me, such things as the shape of plant cells or the repetition and order in which leaves grow from a stem. Pattern is a consistent element in my work; I see patterns as visual clues that can trigger emotions, memories, and stories. My husband is an artist and we are the parents of four creative individuals ranging in age from kindergartener to college student. I have been immersed in the colorful, creative, intense world of children for an extended period of my life, and I believe and hope it has had a lasting effect on me and my work." – Susan Rodriguez

TOP. Round plate with a chartreuse ellipse star pattern and oval dish with a coral spinning flower pattern

MIDDLE. Tear-shaped appetizer plate with a mini tear-shaped dipping dish

BOTTOM. April showers appetizer plate

FAR RIGHT. Tear-shaped serving bowls

Artist:

Chris Stain.

Chris Stain grew up writing graffiti in Baltimore, Maryland, in the mid-1980s. Through printmaking in high school, he adapted stencil-making techniques, which later led to his work in street stencils and international recognition in the urban contemporary art world. Compared at times to the American social realist movement of the 1930s and '40s, Chris's work echoes his upbringing and the people who helped shape his mental and physical landscape. His work illustrates the struggles of the unrecognized and underrepresented individuals of society. Chris currently teaches art part time in New York City and is pursuing a BA in art education. With the help of DRAGO press, he has recently released his first book, *Long Story Short: A Collection of Inspiration.*

TOP. *Brooklyn,* 2009
Hand-cut stencil and spray paint on metal, adapted from a photograph by Martha Cooper, 23" x 26" (58.4 x 66 cm)

MIDDLE. *Boy on Bike,* 2012
Hand-cut Rubylith, screen print on board, hand colored, 16" x 20" (40.6 x 50.8 cm)

BOTTOM. *Family,* 2011
Hand-cut stencil and spray paint on wood, 23" x 26" (58.4 x 66 cm)

TOP RIGHT. *Walking Tall* mural, 2012
New York, NY
Projected stencil and Montana Shock Black spray paint, 8' x 15' (2.4 x 4.6 m)

BOTTOM RIGHT. *Baltimore mural,* 2012
Projected stencil and Rust-Oleum flat black spray paint, 30' x 50' (9.1 x 15.2 m)

Templates

1

Scherenschnitte-Inspired Floor Tiles, *page 29*

Stencils Love Decoupage: Old Wood
and Antique Letters, *page 33*

A Fun Floor Cloth, *page 41*

4

Wall Art: A Pack of Sweet Shelter Dogs, Dog 1, *page 45*

5

Wall Art: A Pack of Sweet Shelter Dogs, Dog 2, *page 45*

6

Wall Art: A Pack of Sweet Shelter Dogs, Dog 3, *page 45*

7

Paper Dolls Please, Dolls, *page 49*

8

Paper Dolls Please, Doll Clothes, *page 49*

9

Fabric Frames: A Pillow Gallery, Frame 1, *page 61*

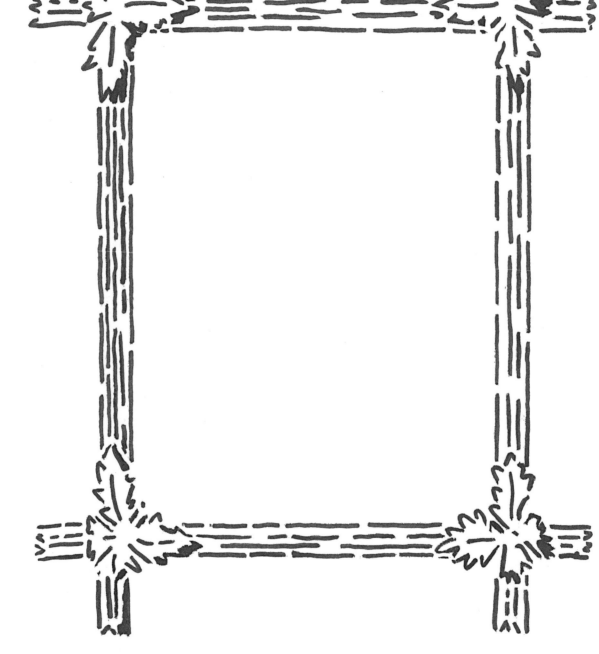

Fabric Frames: A Pillow Gallery, Frame 2, *page 36*

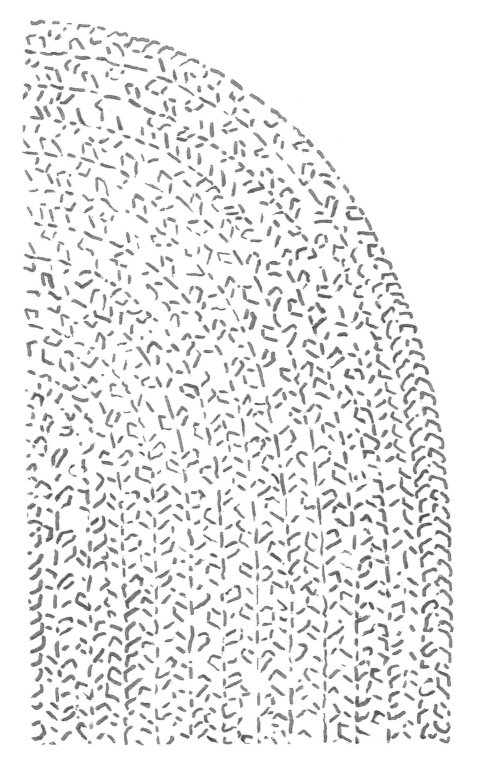

Faux Braided Rag Rug, *page 85*

Dancing in the Rain Shower Curtain, *page 97*

Custom Wallpaper, *page 101*

Artist Directory

Rachel Breen
Minneapolis, MN
rbbreen@yahoo.com

**Broken Crow (John Grider
and Mike Fitzsimmons)**
St. Paul, MN
Stencils@brokencrow.com
www.brokencrow.com

Matt Dixon (aka M-ONE)
Hampshire, UK
mattdixon@gmail.com
www.flickr.com/photos/stencilista

Christian Guemy / C215
Vitry-sur-seine, France
christianguemy@yahoo.fr
www.C215.com

Berry Holz
Minneapolis, MN
berry.holz@gmail.com
www.berryholz.com

Megan Hunter
Perugia, Italy
Getsmarts99@hotmail.com
http://megan-hunter.tumblr.com

Liz Miller
Good Thunder, MN
Liz@lizmillerart.com
www.lizmiller.com

Amy Rice
Minneapolis, MN
amyr@amyrice.com
www.amyrice.com

Susan Rodriguez
San Antonio, TX
ceramicabotanica@live.com
www.ceramicabotanica.etsy.com

Chris Stain
Middle Village, NY
chrisstain@gmail.com
www.chrisstain.com

Resources

Clear Stencil Material and Stencil Burners
E-Z Cut Plastic
P.J.'s Decorative Painting
21 Carter Street
Newburyport, MA 01950
www.pjstencils.com

Commercial Vinyl Wallpaper
Goldcrest Wallcoverings
P.O. Box 245
Slingerlands, NY 12159
www.wallcovering.com

Fabric Fuse
Jo-Ann Fabric and Craft Stores
www.joann.com

Repositionable Spray Adhesive
Krylon Easy-Tack
www.krylon.com

Real Wool Felt
A Child's Dream Come True
www.achildsdream.com

Paintable Wall Paper
Home Depot
www.homedepot.com

About the Author

Amy Rice is a mixed-media artist from Minneapolis, Minnesota. She has been designing and cutting her own stencils for fifteen years. Her stencil artwork has been shown in fine art galleries in the United States, Canada, the United Kingdom, and China.

ACKNOWLEDGMENTS
Thank you to my pack, Matt and Pumpkin, for all their love and support.

Don't miss these other titles from Quarry Books!

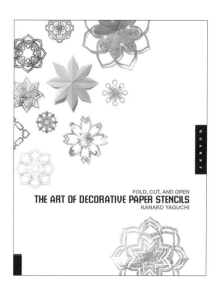

Art of Decorative Paper Stencils
Kanako Yaguchi
978-1-59253-440-1

Print & Stamp Lab
Traci Bunkers
978-1-59253-598-9

Playing with Books
Jason Thompson
978-1-59253-600-9

Playing with Paper
Helen Hiebert
978-1-59253-814-0